BONESTONE & EARTHFLESH TAROT

THE REAWAKENING

by **AVALON CAMERON**

art by **ANA TOURIAN**

BONESTONE & EARTHFLESH TAROT
THE REAWAKENING

© 2025 Avalon Cameron

Artwork © 2025 Ana Tourian

All rights reserved. Except for personal use, no part of these cards or this book may be reproduced, in whole or in part, without written permission from the publisher. These cards are for spiritual and emotional guidance only and are not a substitute for medical advice or treatment. The author's views, within and beyond this publication, do not necessarily reflect those of the publisher. We respectfully request that this content not be used to train AI-generative models or machine learning systems without the publisher's written consent.

Published by Blue Angel Publishing®
10 Trafford Court, Wheelers Hill
Victoria, Australia 3150

info@blueangelonline.com
www.blueangelonline.com

Edited by Peter Loupelis and Jules Sutherland

Designed by Gemma Christensen

Blue Angel is a registered trademark of Blue Angel Gallery Pty Ltd.

ISBN: 978-1-922574-47-3

Designed in Australia. Printed in China with soy-based inks.

TABLE OF CONTENTS

FOREWORD 10

PREFACE AND ACKNOWLEDGEMENTS 12

IN THE BEGINNING 15

The Secrets of Earthflesh 17
Secrets of the Bonestone 31
Building a Relationship with the Bonestone 32
A Bonestone Ritual 39
The Looking Glass: A Selection of Meaningful Tarot Spreads ... 44
Conclusion (From Earth's Depth to Spirit's Light) 52

MAJOR ARCANA 53

0. THE FOOL — Junko 54
I. THE MAGICIAN — Grey One 58
II. THE HIGH PRIESTESS — Huld 62
III. THE EMPRESS — Lady of Leaves 66
IV. THE EMPEROR — Borghild/Wraith 70
V. THE HIEROPHANT — Grandmother 74
VI. THE LOVERS — Sky & Earth 78
VII. THE CHARIOT — Charis the Traveller 82
VIII. STRENGTH — Aadya 86
IX. THE HERMIT — Agafya 90
X. THE WHEEL OF FORTUNE — The Weavers 94
XI. JUSTICE — The Warrior & the Veiled One 98

XII. The Hanged Man — Odin All-Father *102*

XIII. Death — The Fallen Warrior *106*

XIV. Temperance — The Hourglass *110*

XV. The Devil — The Devil *114*

XVI. The Tower — The Mighty Oak *118*

XVII. The Star — Two Eagles *123*

XVIII. The Moon — Kale *127*

XIX. The Sun — The Wild Solar Dance *131*

XX. Judgement — She Who Is Unnamed *135*

XXI. The World — The Oak Guardian *139*

The Bruxa *144*

KINGDOM OF SWORDS 148

Ace of Swords — Quill *150*

Two of Swords — Tella the Traveller *153*

Three of Swords — The Charred Heart *156*

Four of Swords — Battle-Worn Warrior *159*

Five of Swords — Peanut *163*

Six of Swords — Odessa *167*

Seven of Swords — The Shadow Emissary *170*

Eight of Swords — Bel *174*

Nine of Swords — The Beast *178*

Ten of Swords — Earthflesh *182*

Page of Swords — Young Merlin the Apprentice *185*

Knight of Swords — Athena *189*

Queen of Swords — The Morrigan *193*

King of Swords — King Arthur *198*

KINGDOM OF CUPS 202

Ace of Cups — *The Super Blood Moon Eclipse* 204
Two of Cups — *Kindred Spirits* 208
Three of Cups — *Cauldron Sisters* 212
Four of Cups — *Keanu the Fisherman* 216
Five of Cups — *The Elephant Who Mourns* 220
Six of Cups — *The Farmer and his Wife* 223
Seven of Cups — *The Charlatan* 226
Eight of Cups — *Morgana* 230
Nine of Cups — *Peacock Queen & the Elixir of Life* 234
Ten of Cups — *The Lunar Cup* 238
Page of Cups — *Kuan Yin* 242
Knight of Cups — *Lady of the Lake* 247
Queen of Cups — *Yemanja* 252
King of Cups — *Poseidon* 257

KINGDOM OF WANDS 262

Ace of Wands — *The Serpent Fire* 264
Two of Wands — *Flame Bud* 267
Three of Wands — *Cilla* 271
Four of Wands — *The Blessing* 275
Five of Wands — *The Redwood Challenge* 279
Six of Wands — *The Sovereign Self* 282
Seven of Wands — *The Blade Witch* 285
Eight of Wands — *Wild Horse* 289

NINE OF WANDS → *The Green Woman* 293
TEN OF WANDS → *Digger* 297
PAGE OF WANDS → *Iansá* 301
KNIGHT OF WANDS → *Hephaestus* 305
QUEEN OF WANDS → *Marie Leveau* 310
KING OF WANDS → *Sun God Ra* 315

KINGDOM OF PENTACLES 320

ACE OF PENTACLES → *Mandrake Spirit & the Skull of the Old One* 322
TWO OF PENTACLES → *The Rainbow Spider* 326
THREE OF PENTACLES → *Sacred Stone* 330
FOUR OF PENTACLES → *The Lady of Jewels* 334
FIVE OF PENTACLES → *Storm-Swept Family* 338
SIX OF PENTACLES → *Feed the Birds* 342
SEVEN OF PENTACLES → *Oakley* 345
EIGHT OF PENTACLES → *The Sacred Smith* 349
NINE OF PENTACLES → *The Lady of Flowers* 352
TEN OF PENTACLES → *Community* 355
PAGE OF PENTACLES → *Dionysus* 359
KNIGHT OF PENTACLES → *Lilith* 364
QUEEN OF PENTACLES → *Baba Yaga* 368
KING OF PENTACLES → *The Green Man* 373

ABOUT THE AUTHOR 378

ABOUT THE ARTIST 379

The Bonestone & Earthflesh is dedicated to the mystics, the seers, the dreamers, and the weavers. Most of all, it is dedicated to those who watched as Ana and I brought this deck to life. Your support made this possible, your humour made it great, and your trust in us made the Bonestone & Earthflesh pure magic.

— *Avalon Cameron*

Those who contemplate the beauty of the earth find reserves of strength that will endure as long as life lasts ... There is something infinitely healing in the repeated refrains of nature — the assurance that dawn comes after night and spring after winter.

—*Rachel Carson*, Silent Spring

Foreword
(A Seed to Be Planted)

Do you marvel at a mountain's ancient stones, feeling as if you could peer into their deep, secret memories? Or sense that you walk upon the living flesh of Mother Earth herself? *Bonestone & Earthflesh Tarot: The Reawakening* weaves such elemental visions and psychic sympathies into an animistic divination tool imbued with the benediction of land spirits and protective deities. It is truly a magical, mystical deck.

What sets these cards apart is their groundbreaking creation — a fusion of the collective consciousness and modern technology. Forged in real-time with a global community watching via livestream, every card was birthed through the shared energy of like-minded souls tuning in to witness the design and craft of an enchanted tool. Never before has a tarot deck been fully drawn from our interconnected present, channelling the ancient natural magic and mysticism through new media and virtual weaving.

Avalon Cameron, a leading voice in witchcraft, divination, and spirit work, has long inspired tens of thousands with her knowledge, her wisdom, her kindness. She invites us to rediscover the old magic, now vital in our contemporary era. In this deck, she presents herself as both daughter and messenger of our great Earth Mother, tasked with awakening us to the extraordinary surrounding us.

Complementing Avalon's visionary guidance is the art of Ana Tourian. Ana's dynamic, accelerating lines and vibrant colour palette infuse each card with an intensity that breathes life into Avalon's visions. Trained at the Pratt Institute School of Design—the same revered institution that nurtured the iconic illustrator Pamela Colman Smith—Ana channels technical mastery and an empathic resonance, making every card a portal to a living, enchanted realm.

Before our very eyes, a magical marriage of talents unfolded: a community of diviners and tarot readers, united by modern technology, witnessed as spirits from the four quarters were invited to bless and guide the deck's creation. The result is a deck that transcends the ordinary — each card is not merely printed cardstock but a living echo of ancient wisdom and divine inspiration.

— *Benebell Wen, author of* Holistic Tarot

Preface and Acknowledgements (The Vines of Gratitude)

The *Bonestone & Earthflesh Tarot* has been liberated into the world, and many have already been working with the first edition — a true labour of love. What you now hold in your mighty hands is the essence of that labour infused into this new, second edition.

The Bonestone now carries a different energy, yet at its core, it remains the same. Some of the cards have undergone a transformation; the book has been reworked and refined, finalising an almost alchemical evolution. What was once a community-centric project has now become something deeply personal to me. I have breathed new life into this creation, and I truly love the shape it has taken.

As I worked on this second edition, I was also on a journey of healing. I had undergone open-heart surgery and my perspective on the world had shifted. That healing can be found within this powerful iteration of Bonestone — you need only hold the deck in your hands and inhale the magic within.

I carry immense gratitude in my heart. Gratitude for my three little ones, Savannah, Caspian, and Serenity, who continually challenged my focus yet inspired me beyond belief, for each of them is a living, breathing fountain of magic. Gratitude to my beautiful friend and artist Ana Tourian, who never failed to understand my creative vision and gave life to the many imagined scenes floating in my mind. I also extend my deepest thanks to my editor, Peter, whose experience, insight, and dedication helped shape Bonestone into what it is today. And my heartfelt gratitude to my best friend, Erin, for holding my hand as I stepped into this next incarnation of this beloved tarot deck.

With love in my heart for all that I have been blessed to receive,

Avalon Cameron

The Binding

Close all windows, close all doors,
utter not one single word,
let only those of truest blood see,
that which by heart and mind be made seen.

They who dare journey these pages,
this knowledge is secret, handed down
through the ages; with that in sight
and fresh in mind,
these words to you I now do bind.

May the strength of the old enter the new,
this blessing mine I give to you and for those
of you with unfaithful eyes, may your lips be
bound and your tongue be tied.

By the power of earth, air, fire, and water.
From the love of a mother, father,
son, and daughter. Let it be.

In the Beginning, There Was a Library of Leaves ...

In the heart of an unclaimed patch of wilderness, in a place far removed from all that is manufactured, exists Bonestone & Earthflesh — a place rippling with violent confrontations that challenge the modern human construct of how things should be. Here, in this place of vibrant cornucopias, a sovereign legacy is heard. Those listening will find the Sage.

You have taken a willing step into the primeval world of Bonestone & Earthflesh. You are taking a glimpse through the looking glass of sacred, divine landscapes and enduring narratives. Here, you will meet and journey with the hero, villain, lover, and fighter. Those who are sovereign and those who—by choice or circumstance—suffer to a bitter end. This is a world between worlds, a place of discovery, redemption, damnation, and self-realisation. Each character you meet on the path to the inner temple of self-actualisation brings forth a message — an ancient wisdom echoed in the breath of a modern shuffle. In this most hallowed place, you—the mystic seeker—are the weaver.

How will you weave your story? Who from Bonestone will come to your aid? What comfort, logic, or transformative truth will make itself known to you? To know the answers to these questions and infinite others, you will need to reach for the Bonestone. Knock on its door and be invited in.

It is a privilege to read tarot. Whether for the self or another, it is a most sacred act of divine connection. Never forget that.

The SECRETS *of* EARTHFLESH

The deck is Bonestone; the book is called Earthflesh.

This book mirrors the terra-centric theme that envelops the world of Bonestone. Its pages are filled with the alchemy of each card, including their unique narratives, upright meanings, and reversed meanings. Let it be said that this is a 79-card deck because an extra card is included to add an extra touch of magic: *The Bruxa*, who represents the witch, the seer, the wild creative force that is the natural world. Thus, she embodies the essence of the wildcard. *The Bruxa* is an exquisite rogue. You are sure to be taken with her energy.

Astrological Correspondence

I have also listed astrological associations for those who enjoy merging these disciplines with their tarot practice. Integrating astrology with tarot helps you add layers of depth and meaning. Astrology is an ancient esoteric practice that invites you to turn your gaze heavenward and seek understanding hidden within the positions and movements of celestial bodies, such as the planets, stars, the Sun, and Moon, and the interconnected influence that these have on the human spirit.

The Signs

- » **Aries** represents initiative, leadership, and a pioneering spirit. Aries individuals are often seen as confident, action-oriented, and forthright.
- » **Taurus** embodies stability, determination, and a strong connection to the material world. Taureans are known for their practicality and love of comfort and food.
- » **Gemini** represents versatility, curiosity, and communication skills. Geminis are often seen as adaptable, sociable, and fantastic cocreators.

- » **Cancer** embodies nurturing, emotions, and sensitivity. Cancerians are known for their deep emotional connections, protective nature, and perpetually evolving mood.
- » **Leo** signifies creativity, ostentatiousness, and a strong desire for recognition. Leos are often seen as confident and enthusiastic performers.
- » **Virgo** embodies practicality, attention to detail, and a desire for perfection. Virgos are known for their analytical, helpful nature and are masters of acts of service.
- » **Libra** symbolises balance, harmony, and a strong sense of justice. Librans are often seen as diplomatic and fair-minded, driven by a need to please.
- » **Scorpio** embodies intensity, transformation, and a deep connection to the mysteries of life. Scorpios are known for their passion, determination, and their alluring dark side.
- » **Sagittarius** represents adventure, optimism, and a love of exploration. Sagittarians are often seen as adventurous and philosophical. They embody the archetype of the wanderer well.

- » **Capricorn** embodies discipline, responsibility, and a strong drive for success. Capricorns are known for their ambition and determination but habitually move slowly and deliberately.

- » **Aquarius** represents innovation, individuality, and a commitment to social causes. Aquarians are often seen as forward-thinking and humanitarian, the quintessential social butterfly.

- » **Pisces** embodies compassion, intuition, and a deep connection to the spiritual realm. Pisceans are known for their empathy, artistic sensibilities, and spiritual sensitivities.

The Planets

- » **The Sun** represents your core identity, ego, and individuality. It is the most important celestial body in a birth chart because it symbolises the essence of the self. The Sun's sign placement (e.g., Aries, Taurus, etc.) highlights the primary characteristics that a person expresses and identifies with.

- » **The Moon** reflects your emotions, instincts, and subconscious mind. It governs your emotional responses, instincts, and inner emotional world.

The Moon's sign placement reveals how a person processes and expresses feelings.

» **Mercury** governs communication, intellect, and adaptability. It influences how you think, process information, and communicate with others. The sign placement of Mercury indicates one's communication style and mental processes.

» **Venus** relates to love, beauty, and relationships. It signifies how you express affection, value beauty, and approach matters of the heart. Venus' sign placement can provide insights into one's romantic preferences and relationship dynamics.

» **Mars** signifies energy, assertiveness, and drive. It represents how you take action, pursue goals, and assert yourself in various situations. The sign placement of Mars reveals one's approach to challenges and conflicts.

» **Jupiter** indicates expansion, growth, and opportunities. It symbolises abundance, luck, and the quest for knowledge and wisdom. Jupiter's sign placement can provide insights into areas where you seek growth and abundance.

- » **Saturn** represents discipline, structure, and challenges. It symbolises responsibility, accountability, and the need for self-discipline. Saturn's placement in your birth chart points to areas where you may face challenges and lessons to be learned.

The outer planets are associated with generational influences and deeper transformations. They have a more profound and collective impact on a generation of individuals rather than individual personality traits. These planets symbolise societal and spiritual changes, transformation, and evolution.

- » **Uranus** represents innovation, rebellion, and sudden changes in society.
- » **Neptune** governs dreams, intuition, and the spiritual realm. It can also represent illusion and confusion.
- » **Pluto** signifies profound transformation, regeneration, and the cycles of life and death.

How to Use This Information

You can thoughtfully weave astrological knowledge into your tarot readings in many ways. For example, you could pay close attention to the following:

1. Start with the basics. Connect each zodiac sign with its associated tarot card. For instance, Aries connects to *The Emperor*, Taurus to *The Hierophant*, etc.
2. Consider the zodiac sign of the person getting the tarot reading (querent). Focus on the tarot card associated with their zodiac sign to add a personal touch to the reading.
3. Look at the major planets in astrology (like the Sun, Moon, Venus, and Mars) and their meanings. If the querent has a strong planet in their birth chart (like Venus in Aries), pay special attention to tarot cards associated with those planets. But when starting out, focus that knowledge on yourself and your own birth chart.
4. Consider how tarot cards might relate to the querent's zodiac sign or planetary placements when interpreting tarot cards in a spread. For example, if someone is a Leo and draws *Strength* (the card associated with it), it can represent their natural strength and confidence.

5. Record the connections you make between tarot and astrology in your readings. This helps refine your skills over time and see how well they align with the querent's experiences.
6. While astrology can be beneficial, intuition is another key component in tarot readings. Trust your intuition; trust your gut feeling when interpreting cards and their astrological connections.
7. The more you practise combining astrology and tarot, the better you will undoubtedly become at creating meaningful and insightful readings for yourself and others.

Remember, practice makes perfect. There is no need to put extra pressure on yourself when first learning the basics. So, if the idea of weaving astrology into your card readings seems daunting, save it for when you feel more confident in your knowledge of the tarot.

Tarot & Numerology

Tarot integrates beautifully with numerology. The natural numbering system in tarot cards can help add another esoteric layer to your reading.

Numerology is a unique belief system that assigns meaning and significance to numbers, particularly in the context of a person's life, personality, and events. Numerology is based on the idea that numbers carry specific vibrations or energies that offer insights into various aspects of one's life.

In numerology, the core numbers often worked with are:

Life Path Number: The Life Path Number is derived from your birth date and represents your life's purpose and overall path. It is the most significant number in your numerology chart.

Expression Number: This number is calculated using the letters in your full birth name (the name on your birth certificate) and reveals your natural talents, skills, and potential.

Soul Urge Number: The Soul Urge Number, also known as the Heart's Desire Number, is determined by the vowels in your name. It represents your inner desires, motivations, and what truly fulfils you.

Personality Number: This number is calculated using the consonants in your name and reflects the outward traits and characteristics you project to the world.

Destiny Number: The Destiny Number is derived from your full birth name and represents the opportunities and challenges you may encounter in life.

Each numeral from 1 to 9, as well as the Master Numbers 11, 22, and 33, have a unique vibration and symbolism in numerology. Here's a brief overview of the single-digit numbers:

- 1. Independence, leadership, initiation.
- 2. Balance, cooperation, diplomacy.
- 3. Creativity, self-expression, communication.
- 4. Stability, order, practicality.
- 5. Freedom, change, adaptability.
- 6. Nurturing, responsibility, love.
- 7. Introspection, spirituality, analysis.

- » 8. Success, power, abundance.
- » 9. Compassion, wisdom, completion.

Master Numbers:

- » 11. Intuition, spirituality, enlightenment.
- » 22. Master Builder, manifesting dreams into reality.
- » 33. Master Teacher, compassion, and guidance.

When you combine numerology with tarot, you tap into a deeper layer of insight. Each tarot card holds a number that carries its own energy. To use numerology with tarot, simply focus on the digits in the card, whether it's a single number (like 7 in *VII The Chariot*) or a combination (like 12 in *XII The Hanged Man*). If the number exceeds 9, reduce it to a single digit by adding them together (for example, 12 becomes 1+2=3). This number and the card's meaning reveal the underlying numerological energy at play, providing clarity and empowerment in your reading.

Clarifying Numerological Correspondences Between the Major and Minor Arcana

Within many traditional tarot systems, the numbered cards of the Minor Arcana (1–10) are most often associated with the Major Arcana card that shares their cardinal number. For instance, the 2s across the suits (such as the *Two of Wands* or *Two of Cups*) are commonly linked to *II The High Priestess*, as they all embody core themes of duality, receptivity, and intuitive awareness. These correspondences are deliberate and form part of the symbolic framework used in systems like the Hermetic Qabalah and the Golden Dawn traditions.

That said, other interpretive approaches invite us to look a little deeper. When we apply numerological reduction to the Major Arcana, we sometimes find overlapping numbers that suggest further symbolic relationships. For example, when *XI Justice* is reduced (1+1), it resonates with the number 2. In this light, *Justice* offers a complementary lens through which to understand the 2s, enriching the reading with themes of balance, moral consideration, and inner alignment.

This doesn't replace *The High Priestess* as the primary archetype for the 2s; rather, it adds texture to the interpretative process. The initial correspondences are best understood as structural, while these reduced-number resonances can be seen as subtle energetic echoes that offer a deeper, more nuanced understanding when appropriate.

By holding space for both perspectives, we allow for a layered and flexible approach — one that honours tradition while making room for intuitive insight and personal interpretation.

Other Useful Tools

I rather enjoy creating purpose-built, sacred incense blends to cleanse my decks, thus imbuing them with an earthy divinity. I am also fond of selecting crystal keepers to work with my cards. I have found that the continued use of these natural elements creates an overall depth that, simply put, is the equivalent of soul food.

There really is nothing quite like laying out your cards by the flicker of a candle's flame while the heady scent of smouldering incense unfurls in light tufts, dancing a sensual path around you. All the better if you sit before glimmering crystals and water you've collected from a natural place. Such a setting is my happy place.

But do you need all these bells and whistles to work with the cards? No, you do not. You need only the will to explore the cards in a way that feels authentic. We all have our own way of doing things; what is right for me is not necessarily right for you. Please take the time to cultivate your methods mindfully.

The Bonestone is born of witches — there is magic to be found in this deck. To open yourself up to its whispered wisdom is to open yourself up to the magic present within each of the 79 cards and all of life. If you believe your tools to be sacred, then sacred they will be.

Adopt these recommendations practically. Use the herbs listed in each section as a feature in an incense blend, sprinkling powder, charm, tea, or tincture to connect deeper with the card (or to heal from a wound highlighted by a card). I invite you to get creative while working with the natural elements and see where it takes you. You may just find you have a knack for it.

SECRETS *of* the BONESTONE

The Bonestone is a traditional tarot in some ways and non-traditional in others. As a lover of the *Waite–Smith* and Crowley's *Thoth Tarot*, I felt I needed to weave some of these iconic decks' carefully constructed legacies into the alchemical process of creating the *Bonestone & Earthflesh Tarot*.

The backdrop of the Bonestone is verdant, to say the least. This design honours the earth-centric heart that beats a sacred, soulful rhythm deep inside my chest. We all have a sacred song — mine is found in the whispers of the wind, the heady scent of a wet rainforest, the smoky bouquet of a campfire, and the sound of water lapping on rock. The earth is indeed my temple, and I worship her through every fibre of my being. For this reason, I immersed the *Bonestone & Earthflesh Tarot* into a primeval landscape. Bonestone is a place devoid of barriers, with a cross-cultural infusion of magic and story that speaks to the heart and soul. Listen carefully to your inner compass and the ancient whispers of your ancestors, gods, and guides within it.

When it comes to the court cards in particular, this deck encourages readers to look beyond gender. Rather than focusing on whether a figure is male or female, tune in to the archetypal energies that each court card holds. A King represents action, leadership, and authority, while a Queen embodies nurturing, intuition, and creativity. These masculine and feminine forces are universal and exist within all of us. By focusing on these energies instead of gender, you open yourself to deeper, more nuanced interpretations of the court cards.

BUILDING A RELATIONSHIP WITH THE BONESTONE

Some believe that tarot is just a simple stack of cardboard. Others, like myself, believe something a little different. Tarot is a sacred tool that can connect us with divine wisdom. It is of little importance in the grand scheme of things whether you believe this wisdom originates from a guide, deity, or your higher self. What is important is that you see within this lifeless stack of cards a window to the conscious collective — and through it, your soul. If you allow it, tarot can be a confidant, wise counsel, or a friend to assist you in weathering the storms of your life. Tarot can guide you through important decisions and clear the mind lost in the fog of everyday life and the web of energy that we are all entangled in, for good or bad.

The Bonestone is brimming with archetypes. There are no maps, keys, or formal rules to assist you in working with these archetypes. Each card has information for the taking, should you wish to ground into the creative process. The knowledge in this guide is minuscule compared to the ocean of deeply personal experiences you will discover by working directly with this deck.

My advice to you, from my heart to your heart, is to take the leap and embark on your Bonestone & Earthflesh odyssey using your intuition as your primary tool for navigation. Please read the information in this guidebook, but do not allow it to dictate your flow. Your journey with tarot is your own, and the Bonestone is but a chapter in your story. Allow it to inspire you and deepen your adventures.

Be Still with the Deck

Meditate on each card when you feel the call to do so. Choose one every few days, or even every week, and gaze at it. Journal what you see, what catches your eye, what you sense or physically feel. What do you hear, taste, or smell? Write it down; keep a record of it as best you can. You might be surprised at what happens when establishing a dedicated rhythm with this exercise.

Frame It

If confronted with a difficult card, put it in a picture frame and place it on your bedside table. If you do not have a bedside table, place it near your bed. Each time you prepare for sleep, or first thing in the morning when you awaken, you will see the image of that card. When your mind is relaxed, blocks related to the specific card will disintegrate, enabling you to truly connect with the card and its meaning. You can use this tip with any deck or card throwing a spanner in the works.

Journal

You may find it a good idea to keep a journal as you develop your skills with this deck. Journalling is a beautiful practice of creating a written legacy that can be referred to, passed on to another, or perhaps even destroyed in the spirit of cleansing and growth. I also find that writing helps me free emotions from my mind and transfer them to a page, thus unburdening my mental processes. This also assists you in gaining perspective.

By writing things down and taking a step back, we can reach a place of clarity.

Journalling aids you in expressing the deepest facets of yourself, without fear or judgement, in brilliant colour or dark muted tones. The palette or the medium really doesn't matter. What matters is that you felt something enough to express it in your own way, which is beautiful.

Each card has a selection of prompts designed to help you unpack a card's meaning. You might try writing your own if you don't resonate with a prompt. The intention is to allow yourself to speak without fear or judgement. Express yourself through journalling. It's a creative process that enables you to connect with your muse. Question the cards, asking who, what, when, where, why, and how. Draw, paint, write poetry, or copy a quote that inspires and connects you with a particular card. Write down your power thoughts, mantras, moods, or a single word for focus. There is no right or wrong with journalling. Just open a blank journal and go for it. If page fright is a thing for you, use the first page to write the deck title, the date you started, and what you hope to get out of this process. Personally, I use the first few pages as a place to test art products I am interested in using in my journal.

A journal is your creative space, so use it as you see fit and do not allow yourself to be dictated by others in this process. It's very easy to see a beautiful journal or journal page and feel as though yours needs to mimic it. This is not at all the case. Your journal should reflect you and your unique style. It may feel a little awkward at first if you're new to journalling, but that is true of almost everything we try new. There is no pressure and no judgement — you just need to show up to the page and unleash your imagination.

Pathwork Your Way

Pathworking is connecting with a card's meaning by living its adventure. Successful pathworking offers a perfect spiritual exchange — a moment when you are no longer guided by your imagination and instead become spirit-led. The richness of experience that can unfold in a pathworking session is indeed powerful, and the tools required for pathworking are as humble as they are meaningful.

What You Need

- Your *Bonestone & Earthflesh Tarot* deck
- Your journal

- A pen or other preferred writing/drawing implements
- Candle(s) (optional)
- Incense (optional)

The Pathworking Process

1. Find a comfortable and quiet place to sit. Light your candles and incense if you choose to use them.
2. Choose a card based on the energy or image you wish to work with now, or shuffle and pull a card randomly. When you have chosen your card, lay it before you and gaze at it. Please familiarise yourself with its details.
3. Ground and centre yourself, and continue to gaze at the image before you.
4. See the card grow to the size of a doorway, feel yourself get smaller, or feel your consciousness moving closer to the card. Watch as the edges of the card melt away. The barrier between you and the card is no longer there; nothing exists to separate you from the card. Take a breath, steady yourself, and when you are ready, step through the card's threshold and into the image.
5. Take your time interacting with the image of the card. Move through the space and touch, taste,

listen, and see. Accept any information that comes to you during this time — be receptive. Interact with the character(s) in the card, speak to them, ask questions, and listen for their answers. Take your time; there is no need to rush. This is a sacred process to be honoured.
6. When you feel ready, thank the energies that have interacted with you. Ground and centre again and feel your awareness of your body and the space around you growing more potent.
7. When you are once again alert, grab your journal and document your experience. Be sure to take down everything, even the most seemingly insignificant detail. Express yourself fully in your journal. There is magic to be found in a blank page.

Please Note: Do not feel disheartened if your first experience with pathworking isn't all you wanted it to be. Like all things, practice makes perfect. What's important is that you try to document your process. Do the work, and you might just surprise yourself.

What Do You See?

By the time Ana and I had reached the suit of Swords, something strange was apparent to us both, confirmed by others watching the development of this deck. We each saw intimate flashes of deity-like characteristics peeking through each card. We first noted this while colouring the *Two of Swords*. When this presented itself, it opened a floodgate to the rest of the deck. I assure you this was not planned but rather a pure, undiluted act of serendipity.

What can you do with this information? Well, the way I see it, you have two choices: you can choose not to see and bypass this snippet of information altogether (and that would be perfectly alright), or you can take note of who it is that you see peeking out and consider the advice within a reading to be influenced by that energy, archetype, or deity. Honour the prevailing energy which you intuitively feel is prevalent. In other words, work with the gods if you hear their wisdom and feel it to be imbued with a sense of meaning.

A BONESTONE RITUAL

Before you work with the Bonestone, it's essential to establish a connection with it. Since this deck has a strong affinity with the earth, grounding and centring yourself becomes the quickest way to establish that bond. Furthermore, engaging in these mindfulness practices fosters profound awareness and concentration, enabling you to be receptive to the wisdom it offers at any moment.

Once you are grounded and centred, I invite you to create a sacred space. This needn't be a costly or time-consuming task — it's about simplicity and flow. Move in the direction of your spirit, and allow yourself to be guided. Create what feels right for you; adorn in a manner that honours the sacred in you. Let your inspirations and motivations come naturally. Do not force it — to do so would be detrimental to the natural flow of things.

You might consider mirroring the structure of the tarot in your sacred space. Just as there are five distinct sections to the tarot (the Major Arcana and the four suits of the Minor Arcana), so might you consider introducing five items to honour this anatomy. Personally, I have physical representations of earth, air, fire, and water to represent the four cardinal elements of the Minor Arcana. I also have a sacred object that represents spirit. Usually, this object is a bone or a ritual item, but this is not necessary. Each of these five sacred energies is always present in you. If you simply can't be bothered with adornments, sacred spaces, and other such things, then just be 100 percent present in your power, and you will be perfectly fine.

With sacred space established, we move on to cleansing and consecrating your deck. To cleanse is to clean and clear; to consecrate is to make sacred; to dedicate is to imbue with purpose. You may use ethically sourced sage or palo santo, both together, or something a little different. I also encourage you to take a closer look at the beauty and splendour of your own biosphere. Look closely at the botanicals native to your region of the world and try your hand at wild harvesting where it is appropriate to do so.

Sit with your deck for a moment and ask it to guide your hand so you may choose the right way for you. If that approach doesn't work, I would like to offer my way as a means of inspiration only.

I have a loose incense blend that I use for my decks. However, because I developed the Bonestone, and it's tremendously special to me, I created a blend specifically for this deck. You may choose to use it or something like it. I only ask that if you choose to use the Bonestone Blend, you add a little something of your own to the mix to make it yours. This is how we do things in my neck of the wild woods.

Avalon's Loose Smoke Cleanse	Avalon's Bonestone Smoke Cleanse
» Rose *(Rosa spp.)* » Lavender *(Lavandula spp.)* » Frankincense *(Boswellia spp.)* » Bay *(Laurus nobilis)* » Mugwort *(Artemisia vulgaris)* » Sandalwood *(Santalum album)* » Cinnamon *(Cinnamomum verum)*	» Patchouli *(Pogostemon cablin)* » Star anise *(Illicium verum)* » Dragon's blood *(Dracaena spp.)* » Frankincense *(Boswellia spp.)* » Bay *(Laurus nobilis)* » Mugwort *(Artemisia vulgaris)* » Sandalwood *(Santalum album)* » Cinnamon *(Cinnamomum verum)*

Blend with a mortar and pestle until it reaches a nice consistency. Use this loose incense on hot coals to smoke your deck.

The nature of the Bonestone mix is a heady assault on the senses. It possesses a cunning charm that explodes into being when you pound it with a mortar and pestle. The botanicals listed each have magnificent attributes that release the energy of old-world magic. Burn this divine mix on coals by the light of a candle. I recommend a non-toxic red candle to represent Earthflesh.

You are now ready to cleanse and consecrate your *Bonestone & Earthflesh Tarot*. Smoke each of the cards one at a time or all together while you chant, hum, or sing along to the rhythm of a song that alters your mindset. Be sure to check the phase of the moon as you plan your Bonestone ritual. If you are fortunate enough to work your magic under the light of a full Scorpio or Leo moon, then you are truly blessed indeed! These moons had a significant impact on the creation of this deck.

The LOOKING GLASS:
A SELECTION OF MEANINGFUL TAROT SPREADS

I have carefully created a selection of tarot spreads that can be used whenever you require soulful guidance with life's many challenges. Each spread is designed to provide comfort, advice, and support as you navigate the world around you.

Take a deep breath, then ground and centre your energy. Take a second deep and resounding breath, then feel yourself slowly unwinding with each following inhalation and exhalation. Breathe with purpose and meaning. When it feels right, take hold of your deck and shuffle the cards. Focus on your questions, and when you are ready, begin laying out the appropriate number of cards for your chosen layout.

ONE-CARD SPREAD:
PLANT THE SEED OF BLESSINGS

This one-card reading represents the blessing or guidance you seek. It offers insight, inspiration, or a positive message about your intention or question.

For this, you can hold a specific intention or question in your mind as you draw one card. The card you draw will provide a blessing or guidance aligned with your intention, offering you a positive perspective or encouragement to propel you forward on your journey through the day.

Three-Card Spread:
Step into the Waters of Soulful Introspection

Quietening the mind to hear and feel one's true thoughts can be challenging amidst the hustle and bustle of a busy day. So, I invite you to experiment with this spread. It opens the door to a moment of sacred mindfulness, allowing you to honour your thoughts, feelings, and intuition with clarity and compassion. This beautiful and soulful spread helps you dive deep into introspective thoughts and make sense of the proverbial noise if you are tangled in overthinking. As you embark upon this journey of introspection, be deliberate in your engagement with each card's message. Allow the insights they bear to harmonise with the depths of your inner self, creating a symphony of resonance that reverberates through your soul.

» **Card 1: The Root** — Delves into the core of your being, revealing underlying emotions, desires, or subconscious influences that play a significant role in your current state.

» **Card 2: The Reflection** — Encourages you to reflect on your thoughts and actions. It offers insights into how your external experiences mirror your internal world, helping you gain a deeper understanding of yourself.

» **Card 3: The Essence** — Reveals the essence of your soul and authentic self. It offers guidance on aligning your actions and decisions with your authentic nature, promoting a sense of harmony and fulfilment.

Soul's Loving Embrace Spread

This spread is perfect when you need to clarify your thoughts and feelings to ground yourself, centre your heart, and embrace peace. It will help you turn your focus from outside of yourself back onto yourself. This is the perfect spread for encouraging you to channel some much-needed love, kindness, and acceptance into your life because you deserve to be treated with love, kindness, and respect. As you engage with this spread, visualise yourself enveloped in the energies represented by each card, allowing them to fill you with comfort and positivity.

- » **Card 1: Embrace** — The energy of a warm hug, offering comfort and emotional support. It symbolises the love and compassion that surrounds you.

- » **Card 2: Affection** — The affection and care that you can give to yourself or receive from others. It signifies the connections that help you feel cherished and valued.

- » **Card 3: Comfort** — The soothing comfort of understanding and solace. It reminds you that you have a safe space for peace and relaxation.

- » **Card 4: Nurturing** — The nurturing energies in your life. It represents the environments, people, or activities that provide you with a sense of security and nourishment.
- » **Card 5: Radiance** — The positive energy that a warm hug brings, leaving you with a sense of warmth, happiness, and renewed spirit.

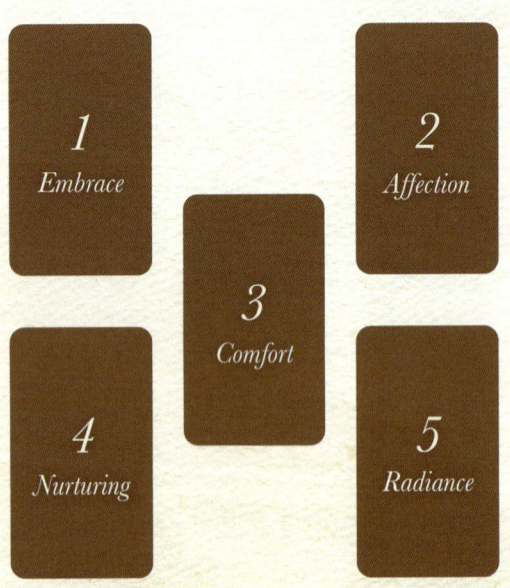

The Path of Primordial Insight Spread

If you feel called to connect with Spirit, I invite you to use this spread. It will ground you in the moment and gently connect you with the realm of Spirit, helping you unearth insights, wisdom, and truth to heal and transform your life. Are you ready for a deep dive into the primal aspects of your sacred self? This spread will help you connect to the hidden power within your inner being, finding courage, wisdom, and inspired guidance through its magic. As you dive deep into the wisdom of this spread, be sure to pay special attention to the rise and fall of your emotions. Tap into the gentle rhythm of your heartbeat. Your heart can be a powerful tool, sifting through the illusion to find the solid and concrete.

» **Card 1: The Veil of the Present** — Your current state and the challenges you are facing right now. It symbolises the hidden aspects of your current situation.

» **Card 2: The Guardian of Challenges** — The specific obstacle or struggle you need to overcome. The guardian offers insight into the energies blocking your path.

- » **Card 3: The Wisdom of the Mystic** — Guidance on the lessons from the challenge. It taps into the mystical wisdom that can be gained from this experience.

- » **Card 4: The Flame Within** — Your inner strengths, talents, and resources aiding you in facing and overcoming the challenge. It symbolises the eternal flame of your spirit.

- » **Card 5: The Weaving Threads** — The external influences affecting your situation. It portrays the threads of fate and how they are interwoven with your journey.

- » **Card 6: The Oracle's Whisper** — Guidance and advice on navigating the challenge and progressing towards personal development. It offers insights whispered by the mystical oracle.

- » **Card 7: The Shifting Constellation** — The potential outcome of your efforts and the direction your personal development journey may take. It reveals the shifting patterns of destiny and the stars that guide you.

1. The Veil of the Present
2. The Guardian of Challenges
3. The Wisdom of the Mystic
4. The Flame Within
5. The Weaving Threads
6. The Oracle's Whisper
7. The Shifting Constellation

CONCLUSION
(FROM EARTH'S DEPTH TO SPIRIT'S LIGHT)

Thus, I welcome you to the world of Bonestone & Earthflesh. It is a profound honour to share this sacred space with you. As you journey through these cards and their messages, may the wisdom you uncover remain forever in your wild heart, reminding you of your own innate magic.

Be as bold as you are blessed,

Avalon Cameron

MAJOR ARCANA

JUNKO

0. The Fool

The Spirit seeks experience and invites you to open up to the unbridled world and the myriad of new experiences that await. Be brave enough to leap into the great unknown.

IN A READING

A potential for adventure lies ahead. Whether that means embarking on a project you have no realised skill set for or embracing a free-spirited approach to life, *The Fool* heralds a time of beginnings and grand adventures masquerading as an innocent step that could have far-reaching consequences. It is also a great reminder to loosen up a little and stop taking life so seriously — there is a time and a place for the serious and the dedicated.

Be spontaneous, express yourself freely and creatively, and embrace fully what comes your way. This is a card of trust and belief. At times, that means the belief in the seemingly impossible. To Junko, there is no such thing as impossible, only grand adventure. By fully embracing this energy, you call into being the spirit of adventure, thus ushering in a new era where trust and a true leap of faith will open you to a myriad of new possibilities.

Reversed

This card can also indicate a time of foolhardy escapades fraught with the arrogance of simple naïveté. As a dreamer, Junko can get caught up in unrealised dreams based on unrealistic ideas so flamboyant that plans naturally go awry. This can result from a superficial outlook that lacks clarity and substance.

When *The Fool* appears reversed in your reading, you are called upon to ground and centre. Now is a time to be mindful, understand the consequences of your actions, and assume the responsibilities you have been shirking. It may also be time to answer that difficult question that has been lingering in the back of your mind. Accept the consequences of your actions with grace and maturity. Take charge of your responsibilities, and by doing so, you will demonstrate good character and healthy respect for yourself and those impacted by your behaviour.

Narrative

Junko is the eternal living spirit, the very expression of life at its purest and most vulnerable. In the primeval forests of Bonestone, she has chosen to experience life as a divine, sacred vessel bursting with raw, primal power. Every day, she walks to the grand oak guardian and asks the same question, "What is this song that calls to me in the deepest of nights?" The grand oak guardian yawns open its gnarled trunk, revealing a perfect view of the cosmos. A blaze of colour and twinkling light is so impossibly beautiful that she becomes enthralled, eyes alight, heart pounding, breathy, excited.

Junko's curiosity will result in her taking a most-fated step. One which will transform her eternal spirit into matter and allow her the pleasure and pain, joy, and sorrow of a perfectly imperfect human adventure. Junko is the mystical seeker, the explorer, the adventurer. Her story is, and has always been, to take that first step and experience it completely, no matter the outcome. This is her sacred duty, and she takes it with ease, unaware of the dangers that lie ahead.

Correspondences

- **Astrology:** Uranus
- **Numerology:** 0, 22

Journal Prompts

- When was the last time you were genuinely excited?
- When did you surrender your fear and take a leap of faith?
- When have you found yourself filled with a desire for a new experience?
- When have you failed to accept the call of the unknown?

Grey One
I. THE MAGICIAN

GREY ONE

I. The Magician

Harness knowledge and skill, and combine to create mastery. Then apply that mastery well, and the power to manifest will be yours.

IN A READING

Examine closely the root of your dexterity and put it to good use. You have power in this situation, perhaps more than you think. Only by harnessing your vast pool of resources can you direct that power to assist you in achieving your goals. Focus is paramount in this situation, prompting you to apply your knowledge to constructive projects. This is a bold reminder that the world is your greatest source of wisdom.

This card also brings the genuine power of creation to your awareness. Harness this power. Relinquish the desire for control and assume the role of the sacred bridge, channelling spirit into matter, thus affecting genuine change. By doing so, you act from your divine core, a place of pure authenticity from which sacred change is born.

It may also remind you of a well of untapped power getting restless. Ground and centre yourself often to avoid a build-up of restless energy. Indulge your creative side in an active capacity. Explore what stokes the sacred flame of your creative fire. Unleash your magic upon the world and watch in pure splendour as it reshapes your reality for the better. Be as bold as you are brave!

Reversed

When *The Magician* appears reversed in your readings, he calls your motives into question. You may have behaved rashly, channelling vast amounts of ego instead of wisdom. There is a cockiness to be contained here and the understanding that you do not know it all. You are not acting with a clear purpose. Your emotions might be running too high, and your motivations questionable. There is a potential for destruction here. Grounding and centring your energy is paramount — less is more. Listen rather than speak, and slowly but surely, you will reconnect with the deep well of wisdom inside of you. Take a moment to examine your motivations carefully. Ensure you are motivated by wisdom, integrity, respect, compassion, and creativity in its purest form.

You have a creative block stopping you from accessing your power and affecting how you create change. Pay attention to what afflicts you at this very moment, whether person, job, place, or thing. See beyond the illusion and straight to the crux of the matter. Channel your mental prowess into strong action, which, when applied, generates the power to break down your creative blocks, leaving you with a fountain of raw creative energy at your disposal.

Narrative

They call him 'Grey One', a name echoing his antiquity. In his dimly lit chamber, he meticulously works on his newest creation: a sphere of colour, iridescent and dragon-shaped, illuminating the room. His skilled hands channel centuries of knowledge, recalling a time when he was young and foolish, yet happy.

The Grey One knows the importance of seeing beyond illusions. He understands that the light before him emanates from an ancient place within, present in all living things. His age-softened features carry memories and teachings. A wise and humble man, his reputation is legendary, yet here he is, refining his craft and about to release a dragon.

Correspondences

» **Astrology:** Mercury
» **Numerology:** 1

Journal Prompts

» Where is your source of power?
» What motivates you in this moment?
» Where in your body can you feel your power flow?
» What is most sacred to you?

HULD

II. The High Priestess

Connect with the profound knowing hidden in the deepest parts of your inner being. This is the pathway for initiation into the feminine mysteries. Do not be seduced by superficial illusions.

In a Reading

This card signals a time of intuitive development and profound inner growth. Your psychic gifts make their presence felt deep in the core of your being, and a sense of knowing envelops you in an inexplicable way. You need time to process and recalibrate. Allow yourself that time by taking care of your needs and listening to what your mind, body, and spirit are telling you. Pay particular attention to your dreamscape and consider any signs you notice. By doing so, the synchronicities will point to a more favourable outcome to your question.

The presence of *The High Priestess* also introduces you to the powerful dark feminine and, with it, the mystique of the inner world. With that deep knowing comes a desire to explore its source. This desire for exploration is both necessary and revolutionary. You find that the call of the mystic arises, leading you down an occult path in search of deeper truths. There, you will discover a well of history and power that you can assimilate in order to gain confidence and clarity within the grand scope of your intuitive gifts.

Reversed

Should this card appear reversed in your reading, it warns of deceit, duplicity, the absence of crucial information, or information that may be veiled in lies to the detriment of the seeker. The necessity for clarity and a deeper understanding of the crux of the matter is paramount. It is an indicator of untapped potential, as well as a block in your psychic and spiritual development. The exploitation of your gifts is yet another matter to consider. Understanding your limits and enforcing your boundaries is necessary in such situations. Likewise, it is important to respect the boundaries of others and refrain from using your psychic talents on another without their consent. Never assume that because you know, so too should they. And lastly, excessive time spent in the veiled world leads to a distortion of reality and a feeling of being disconnected, misunderstood, and sometimes even haunted. Grounding, centring, and re-evaluating both your approach and your motivations is paramount in remedying the effects of spirit on the psyche. This practice will work wonders in securing a clear and present mind. Common sense and reason will aid you in seeing through any confusion and getting straight to the heart of a matter that demands your attention and complete clarity of mind.

Narrative

Huld sees all. She sees beyond the facade and the carefully constructed veneer of humanity. Forever lost in the world of foresight and premonition, Huld walks the veiled world at the behest of those seeking her gifts. Her strength is married to her mystique and to a skill that leaves those with safeguarded secrets quivering in their skin. Huld does not boast, nor does she speak out in attack or defence of others, for this is not the function of an oracle. Her gift is knowing the deepest of truths and sharing that which is necessary, when it is necessary. Huld is composed and formidable in her own right. Those who know of her know all too well the consequences of disrespecting the oracle.

Correspondences

- **Astrology:** Moon
- **Numerology:** 2

Journal Prompts

- What is deep within you?
- Where do your thoughts linger the most?
- What does 'intuition' mean to you?
- When did you last experience the feeling of profound knowing?

LADY OF LEAVES

III. The Empress

Step into a time of creativity and abundance. Life is offering you the opportunity to birth your greatest passions and pleasure.

IN A READING

This is a time of growth and fertility of spirit through pure beauty and human emotion. Now is the time to plant the seeds of creation and feed each with purpose, intention, and unconditional love. Connect with the archetype of mother, lover, and grand creatrix. Birth new opportunities and cultivate new pathways for yourself to explore. Connect with your creative centre and allow yourself to experience a phase of passion in your life, a phase of unfurling soulful radiance that honours the sacred feminine.

Bring your attention to the necessity of self-love and self-care. Take a moment to connect with your centre and see if you are in a state of optimum health and wellness. To nurture your body is to give it love and attention. This is indeed a sacred act that leads to profound honouring of mind, body, and spirit. On a larger scale, *The Empress* points to environmental care and nurturing the planet. Consider your carbon footprint, and take stock of your environmental behaviour. Only then can you truly understand your impact on the natural world. Once you have such a valuable understanding, you can then make the most necessary of changes.

Reversed

When *The Empress* appears reversed in your reading, it suggests a time of unfruitfulness, where inner growth is stifled to the detriment of the creative spirit. A repressive energy is present in your life, indicating a phase of inner escape and a lack of physical intimacy with oneself and others. Laziness and co-dependency may affect your relationships, causing your sense of security to feel threatened. In order to bring healing to the sacred feminine, connect with a practice that stimulates your creativity. Connect with this practice often, daily if possible, and by doing so, you will begin to feel a positive shift in your feminine energy.

This card reversed could also alert you to a phase of disconnection with the sacred feminine, leading to issues with motherly archetypes, both without and within. Problems with female fertility and unhealthy expression of emotion are also indicated. Destructive behaviour is called into question, particularly during times of emotional upheaval. Examine your motivations to pinpoint destructive patterns. Shadow work may be called for. Take a moment to soothe your emotions and connect with your heart centre. Only then can you step into a space of clarity and peace.

Narrative

The Great Earth Mother, our Lady of Leaves, is the embodiment of the natural world. A cornucopia of sound and colour, she is the oldest of deities — sacred and wise, powerful and deadly. To harm her creation will anger her, and when angered, she will thwart. She has wiped out entire villages and the many tribes that lived within. As a mother, she is kind and all giving, granting unconditional love to her children. As a lover, she is formidable, sensual, emotional, and boldly authentic. She spares no part of herself when she chooses to give of herself.

Correspondences

» **Astrology:** Venus
» **Numerology:** 3

Journal Prompts

» Where in your life are you most fertile?
» What is your passion?
» How can you surrender to beauty at this time in your life?
» What does your carbon footprint look like right now?
» What is blocking you right now?

Borghild/Wraith
IV. THE EMPEROR

BORGHILD /WRAITH

IV. The Emperor

Step into a decisive leadership role and become a governing authority in your life. Discipline, courage, and order are required to maintain firm boundaries.

IN A READING

Connect with the primal masculine force for the purpose of establishing structure and order in your life. Confidence and authority are required in the pursuit of a cause that captures your focus right now. Your capacity for leadership is being called on to ensure successful outcomes in projects you may be working on.

When you feel stuck, find clarity in a father figure or feel the call to look deeper towards a more ancient wisdom. Look for successful examples of your situation to adopt a winning strategy. Being organised is imperative and will ensure a meticulous plan. Find stillness in the chaos and calm yourself to avoid rash action, and know that by doing so, you will bring a greater sense of peace into your life. A greater sense of peace leads to a greater sense of clarity, thus providing you with a clear plan of action that can be applied to your current situation.

Courage is required at this time, as you are being called on to hold your position in defence of your honour. With *V The Emperor* in a prominent position in your reading, connect with the type of grounded strength that leads you to a safe and secure space for those in your care. Your stability, skill, and power are being called on to help temper the increased responsibilities you are experiencing.

Reversed

The Emperor reversed warns you of a propensity to overreact, make harsh judgements or jump to conclusions without all the necessary details required to fully grasp the complexity of the situation. Perhaps you're taking a dominant stance in a situation that could result in the oppression of another. Take stock of your relationships to determine whether you are taking your dominance too far. By paying close attention to your actions, words, and attitudes, you will become a more conscious and respectful communicator.

Alternatively, this reversed card indicates a softening of dominant energy, bringing about a more subdued approach. It may refer to someone who has trouble asserting dominance when the situation demands it. If you are having difficulty enforcing your boundaries, then the solution is to work on your self-worth. What of yourself do you value? Now is the right time to ask yourself this question. Until you know what you value, you won't be able to defend it with the courage and conviction needed to maintain your integrity.

Narrative

Borghild was born on a stormy night amid thunder and lightning. Her home was struck by lightning and erupted into flames, and she was born in a crown of fire. Daughter of a strong mother and battle-worn father, and sister to five brothers, she was raised to be strong and capable. Her inner strength and cunning emerged early, moving through the world as if guided by the old ones. She bested foes in battle with silent ease, finding calm before each strike. As she grew, so did her mastery of combat. The townsfolk, fearful of her strange ability, whispered about her ice-blue eyes and haunting gaze. No longer known as Borghild, she became the 'Chieftain Wraith', guided by the legendary chieftains that preceded her. She was the gods' weapon, sent to enforce the law, keep peace, and defend until death.

Correspondences

- » **Astrology:** Aries
- » **Numerology:** 4

Journal Prompts

- » Where can you assert more dominance?
- » How can you improve your organisational skills?
- » What situations in your life could benefit from more structure?
- » How can you improve your capacity to set and communicate boundaries?

GRANDMOTHER

V. The Hierophant

Grandmother
V. THE HIEROPHANT

Guided by a wise teacher, you will gain the tools and spiritual knowledge needed to navigate your situation. Enriching your life with timeless meaning leads to profound personal discovery.

In a Reading

You are being called to walk a more traditional path, one of wisdom and truth. Although appearing conventional from the outside, it holds an ancient wisdom that should never be mistaken for archaic. There is an inherent nobility in the old ways. By walking this seemingly conventional path, you will gain more worlds than you think.

The wise crone leads you down a path of truth and profound personal discovery. If you fear conformity, you should question why. Grandmother does not seek to repress your spirit. She simply wishes to show you a way through your situation, a way through the thicket.

With the aid of such a teacher, you will be given the tools to assist you on your path and taught to use them for the benefit of yourself and those around you. Their proper application will help you transform your circumstances and instigate a healing evolution within. Make good use of the tools you have, and build something of traditional value and timeless meaning that enriches your life in countless ways. Look to tradition for inspiration.

This card also suggests that spiritual knowledge is necessary to understand your current situation better. To access this knowledge, you must be prepared to walk the path of truth-seeker in search of the wise crone. When found, she will guide you to a deeper spiritual understanding that will ultimately lead you through the path of the unknown so that you may access your own sovereignty.

Reversed

In reverse, *The Hierophant* refers to the concealment of crucial knowledge. If this is the case, acknowledge the abuse of authority here, as it is detrimental to spiritual and emotional wellbeing. In turn, it causes confusion and a deep sense of misalignment. Knowledge is power, and hoarding such a power for good or ill is simply unacceptable and may be viewed as a manipulation of facts.

Furthermore, there is a pressure to conform, an ego-driven push from someone in a position of spiritual power who should know better. There is no single 'right way' — each way is unique for each seeker. Imposing your views on another at this time will result in crossing spiritual boundaries and disrespecting another's right to an autonomous practice. If you are doing this, you need to question your motives.

Alternatively, this card reversed asks you to break the mould and experience the cultivation of truth through a self-guided odyssey. Step off the well-worn path in search of non-traditional learning. By doing so, you gain personal experience based on your actions and choices, arising from trial and error. Be patient with yourself, and you will possess true wisdom born from authentic lived experiences.

Narrative

Her people call her 'Grandmother', for she surrendered her name to nature a lifetime ago. She is the keeper of ancient wisdom handed down over many lifetimes. She holds the space of the sacred crone, the wise elder of her people. They turn to her every day for all manner of things— to heal, understand, wed, bury, enchant, and guide. She presides over every rite of passage and sacred ceremony. It is Grandmother who guides those into the realm of spirit. It is she who teaches the old ways. She is responsible for ensuring that the ancient legacy of a fading world is passed along to a worthy student.

Correspondences

» **Astrology:** Taurus
» **Numerology:** 5

Journal Prompts

» What does 'tradition' really mean to you?
» Where in your life have you been forced to conform?
» If you were standing before the wise crone, what would she say to you?
» When have you been called to break tradition?

SKY & EARTH

VI. The Lovers

You will find passion, duality, choice, and understanding through sacred union that leads to harmonious co-creative partnerships and enduring connections.

IN A READING

When *The Lovers* appears in your reading, it suggests a growing attraction to a person, place, or thing — an almost irresistible pull to a state of being that may be foreign to you. This call is being spurred by a desire for balance. Uniting your masculine and feminine aspects will fuel your passion project and create better outcomes.

When the call of *The Lovers* is felt, it signals a time of surrender. Let go of resistance and recalibrate so you can achieve a state of understanding where all motives are clear. By embracing sacred surrender, you connect with a sense of openness, clarity, flow, and greater purpose.

Fostering connection will become essential to the health of anything you have in the works. If that happens to be a relationship, then be sure you are both on equitable footing, and your choices are crystal clear. Knowing where you stand with another solidifies a vital sense of security, and from this, a solid foundation is born, ensuring that anything you choose to build will endure.

Reversed

The Lovers reversed indicates a lack of choice and an unwillingness to commit to anything, resulting in a lack of union and a push-and-pull of power. This rivalry results in a collapse of amicability, thus affecting the outcome of any situation resting on the union of opposites.

It also warns of a toxic cycle of jealousy and distrust, which fuels temptations. Fidelity may be questioned as choices become more complicated, resulting in feelings of betrayal. Once trust is broken, there is very little hope of establishing a healthy connection. However, if you are both committed to healing, your connection can be restored with time, effort, and conscious action, potentially resulting in a more assertive, more respectful, and healthy bond.

Narrative

"As above, so below." The union of Sky and Earth was written in the heavens. For too long did the Sky God long for the touch of another. Craving intimacy and connectedness, he would gaze upon the beautiful Earth and her abundant, flourishing garden. He yearned for her touch and kiss. He yearned for her to look up just once so he could see her smile, a smile meant only for him. Little did he know that Earth yearned for him, for his touch, for his kiss, for his gentle caress. If only she could reach out to him, if only he could see her smile, a smile meant only for him.

Alas, the gods would not allow it … until one day, the sadness of both could be as seen as it was felt. Sky became grey and stormy, and Earth grew dry and barren. The gods convened to discuss a solution to this problem. Finally, they agreed that every day, at sunrise and sunset, Sky and Earth would meet. There, in the in-between space, the gods would slow time for their union, turning an hour into a day so that they may experience time together. As soon as the decree was given, Sky cleared, and Earth bloomed. The moment they met, time—as promised—stood still for them.

Correspondences

- » **Astrology:** Gemini
- » **Numerology:** 6

Journal Prompts

- » What does it feel like when you balance the masculine and feminine aspects of yourself?
- » In what ways do you find yourself being cooperative in different situations?
- » What are you yearning for?
- » What do you look like when in love?

CHARIS THE TRAVELLER

VII. The Chariot

Take pride in your success and the willpower that led you to travel down a great many roads, gifting you with divine knowledge and a world of experience.

IN A READING

This card indicates a situation where you need to gain mastery. Employing your character and willpower leads you to a personal victory. With an iron will and a little effort, you can overcome any obstacles in your path, but you must be diligent and focus on what is important.
It is also a great reminder to pay it forward. If you are currently basking in a state of victory, remember to give a little back. Understand that many individuals have contributed to your personal success. Adopting an open heart and a positive mindset will go a long way in helping

you carry forward the best of your path, leaving behind what no longer serves you.

Travel is another key aspect of this card. Movement and transportation become important, so check the integrity of your travel plans and ensure your chosen mode of transportation is mechanically sound.

Reversed

You may be feeling lost and uncertain of which way to go. When *The Chariot* appears reversed, it's warning you of stagnation and a fundamental lack of direction. If this is the case, stay calm and avoid any rash decisions. Take a moment to find your bearings. Reach for your wisdom and experience to help bring your path back into focus and regain control over the situation.

It's also a warning of transport issues and a change in travel plans. A lack of direction and inability to take charge may result in cancelling any plans involving travel. Find your inner resolve. Take the reins and secure a positive outcome for yourself. By doing so, you regain control of the situation, and a positive outcome will emerge through diligent effort and close attention to detail.

On a positive note, the reversed *Chariot* may indicate that you've finally reached a point of being 'fed up'. This may be due to pure exhaustion of will and a desire to desist from investing any more energy into a situation. This is a time of rest and recuperation to fill your proverbial cup. You cannot draw from an empty well; gather your strength so you can meet your challenge with renewed purpose and vigour. Then, you can achieve a positive and fruitful outcome.

Narrative

For the longest time, Charis was consumed by wanderlust — the desire to see all, learn, love, and conquer the roads, meeting many a soul. She built her caravan at age 15 and set out on the road against her parents' wishes. Everywhere she ventured, she would learn and teach. She shared all her knowledge and passions with others, including her fascination with tarot, astronomy, healing, and communicating with horses. While there were many who did not quite understand, Charis made peace with the road and understood one fundamental truth — travel changes one's circumstances considerably. So, she travelled to widen her perspective on matters much bigger than herself. She found herself over and over again, triumphing over stereotypes. She took charge of her life and amassed knowledge. She grew with the years until the road to everywhere was her most cherished home.

Correspondences

- » **Astrology:** Cancer
- » **Numerology:** 7

Journal Prompts

- » What are you heading towards right now?
- » What is your true path?
- » In which areas of your life must you take charge?
- » What can you do to pay it forward?
- » When did you last taste success?

Aadya
VIII. STRENGTH

AADYA

VIII. Strength

Embrace courage, compassion, and self-control. There is mercy to be found within the realm of true power. Be determined and demonstrate dignity and fortitude of character.

IN A READING

When *Strength* appears, it urges you to find your centre. Circumstances unfold that prove challenging, so self-control is called for. Connect with your power, passion, and determination to overcome challenges and assist in healing what has been fractured. Practising soul retrieval may prove beneficial to you — a shamanic practice focusing on repairing your fragmented soul, thus bringing about a state of wholeness and healing. You cannot find your true centre without first attaining a sense of wholeness.

A call for mercy is also a sign of strength. Conduct yourself with honour and virtue. Should you, or someone close to you, be unable to reach a state of sobriety, then employ compassion and kindness as opposed to forceful and controlling judgement.

Reversed

Are you being pushy or aggressive? *Strength* reversed asks you to question your current approach. Brute force is not advised and will lead to complications. Meditation, pathworking, and journalling help you connect with your centre and, through it, your authentic power. You are also encouraged to examine your health. Abstaining from junk foods and stimulants and adopting a more holistic view of wellness is recommended. Making the necessary adjustments to your diet and lifestyle will result in positive outcomes that lead you down the path of healing, where a new and brighter chapter of your life awaits.

Narrative

Aadya was a peaceful child who loved animals, and they found peace in her company. Her life was challenging: a drunk father and a mother with a broken spirit. Aadya mourned her mother's lost inner strength. As the chaos of her parents' arguments erupted daily at home, Aadya would flee to a cliff's edge, sitting in perfect stillness in search of peace.

Over time, Aadya's visits to the cliff led to encounters with mighty beasts — panthers, snakes, bears, and elephants all revealed themselves to her. These interactions led to a great inner transformation as each creature shared its wisdom with her. Soon, she was able to draw the power of each beast into herself.

At 17, Aadya was returning from the market when she heard her mother's blood-curdling scream. Dropping her basket, she ran home to find her father strangling her mother. Aadya roared like a bear, charged, and bit her father. Horrified, he fell back, seeing her snake-like fangs and yellow eyes. "I will never forgive or forget this," Aadya boomed. "Leave now and never return!" This command he obeyed.

Correspondences

» **Astrology:** Leo

» **Numerology:** 8

Journal Prompts

» How are you strong?

» If you could assume the form of any powerful animal, what would you choose to be?

- » When was the last time you *really* roared?
- » In what way do you demonstrate compassion in your daily life?
- » What do honour and virtue mean to you?

AGAFYA

IX. The Hermit

Seek out solitude and disconnect from the noise. Only then can you find the peace you need. Remember, truth is hidden in the quiet and contemplative moments of life.

In a Reading

When *The Hermit* appears, it urges you to take a beat and rest a moment. Seek out healthy solitude to clear your mind and gain perspective. This is a great time to consider participating in a retreat, going on a social-media cleanse, or creating a safe space and sanctuary in your home. There is wisdom to be found in quiet moments, but in order to achieve such quiet states, one must be prepared to embrace sacred selfishness — setting boundaries and placing your needs ahead of others'.

Illumination will come from time spent in meditation and taking inner journeys. Guard your higher thoughts, particularly if your mind feels busy or cluttered. It is up to you to find your inner temple and connect with it completely. This card also introduces you to a potential mentor who will guide you and offer wise counsel when needed. A period of maturity is about to unfold, where what you genuinely need and want appears vastly different.

Reversed

In reverse, this card indicates a time of chaos, where the mind will have little chance of experiencing quiet. Or, you are in a position that requires wise counsel, yet your sphere of consciousness is devoid of suitable guidance — alternatively, you may have found wise counsel but are not taking it to heart. It can also be a sign of immaturity, leading to ignorant, arrogant, and self-centred interactions that have you appearing incredibly incapable. There may be a slight loss of confidence in your character and capabilities. You are well advised to hold your tongue before any more damage is done.

Alternatively, *The Hermit* reversed could call you to unplug from the noise of social media and the overall loudness of the digital world. Recalibrate to the rhythm of quiet things and reach for peace. When you consciously reach for peace, you will find it in simple pleasures that help ground and centre you.

Narrative

Agafya is a tribute to the great Siberian woman who lived in the Siberian *taiga* her entire life, living off the land and fending for herself. She was born into a family seeking sacred isolation during turbulent times. Raised on the land with her family, she relied on it day after day for everything. Eventually, and quite naturally, her once-large family dwindled until, at last, it was just her. There, in the isolation of a savage wilderness, she remained hidden from the world, in solitude and detached from all society. Agafya became a part of the wilderness. Bonded to the land, she was at peace. She found discipline, wisdom, and sanctuary in her unique circumstances.

Correspondences

- » **Astrology:** Virgo
- » **Numerology:** 9

Journal Prompts

- » How often do you seek solitude?
- » What do you need to do all on your own?

- » Could you benefit from receiving guidance from a mentor?
- » What have you been ignoring?
- » What does sacred selfishness look like to you?

The Weavers
X. THE WHEEL OF FORTUNE

THE WEAVERS

X. The Wheel of Fortune

Embrace the spinning wheel and, with it, the winds of change. A cycle is coming to a close, and another is about to begin.

IN A READING

Luck is at last on your side because *The Wheel of Fortune* signifies a change in the winds. Be on the lookout for synchronicity and serendipity, for both are likely during the time represented by this card.

A fortuitous cycle begins, ushering in a time of change where success and opportunity are likely. The celebration of annual events may be at the forefront of conversations right now. If this is the case, you are advised to breathe fresh life into the tried and true approach of previous years. Go beyond your usual habits and explore and master new ones. Try your hand at a different culinary dish or creative, fun, interactive activities.

The Wheel of Fortune also indicates that the situation you find yourself in is out of your hands. Fate is at play, and destiny is something to ponder. You may even be having moments of déjà vu. It is time to surrender to the divine flow. Surrendering control allows you to step back and view situations from insightful new angles. When you're not caught up in the throes of tightly gripped micromanaging tactics, you see solutions or opportunities you had missed. Surrendering control doesn't mean doing nothing; rather, it's an active choice to allow life to unfold. Why fight against the current when you can simply go with it?

Reversed

An unfortunate change in cycles is upon you, and misfortunes may lead to failure. *The Wheel of Fortune* reversed signals a time to loosen up and change the status quo. You may have inadvertently fallen into a rut. If so, now is the time to wise up and play by the rules of the Weavers. Should you identify a cycle of abuse, gain support from a qualified professional. Alternatively, *karma* may be ready to bite you on the butt. Assert your willpower and focus on what is important. This is a time of flux, so embrace the strange movements of things and watch as life slowly repositions itself into a new cycle. There is little you can do here besides simply go with the flow.

Narrative

The Norns of Norse mythology—Urd, Verdandi, and Skuld—are timeless weavers of fate, guardians of the threads that bind all existence. These enigmatic sisters dwell at the roots of Yggdrasil, the World Tree, whose sprawling branches cradle the nine realms within their ancient embrace. At the base of this sacred tree, where the past, present, and future converge, the Norns ceaselessly weave the intricate tapestry of life. Their craft is a sacred act of creation, an orchestration of destinies spun from the very essence of time. With her deep knowledge of the past, Urd draws upon memories and echoes of what has been. Verdandi, poised in the ever-changing present, intertwines the now with threads of possibility. And Skuld, gazing into the mysteries of what is yet to come, adds the final strands, sealing the fates of gods and mortals alike. Their work is as inexorable as time itself. Unbiased and unyielding, they weave with a hand that neither judges nor favours, their presence felt in every twist of fortune and turn of fate. In their loom, the fabric of reality is fragile and indomitable, a reminder of the interconnectedness of all things and the eternal dance between what was, what is, and what shall be.

Correspondences

- » **Astrology:** Jupiter
- » **Numerology:** 1

Journal Prompts

- » What is luck?
- » What is the difference between *karma* and *dharma*?
- » What does the term 'fortune' mean to you?
- » What do you think sits at the centre of the Wheel?

The Warrior & the Veiled One
XI. JUSTICE

THE WARRIOR & THE VEILED ONE

XI. Justice

Through the honesty and righteousness of decisions, the path unfolds with accountability, fostering peace, agreements, and the gentle art of diplomacy.

In a Reading

Call into question the subject of sacred balance. You cannot put off making important decisions any longer. Are you being as fair with yourself as you are with others? If not, now is the time to remedy this. The decision to use your warrior or peace-bringer aspect is yours to make. Assess your motivation and ensure exchanges are fair. Are you giving more than you get or getting more than you give?

Justice also extends itself to the area of health. Are you currently in balance physically, emotionally, and spiritually? Have you been nurturing one area of your life more than others? Acknowledge both the balances and the imbalances, and make a plan to bring back a state of harmony to your wellness journey. Execute your strategy with grace, the spirit of experimentation, and a little flexibility. Watch on as, little by little, your situation aligns with your new rhythm.

A legal situation requires careful consideration. Remember, the justice system is a human invention and doesn't refer to divine or sacred justice but to a modern view of justice as determined by society. *Justice* can suggest a fair outcome and just results. Prioritise open communication, explore alternative solutions collaboratively, and be proactive in finding common ground. With a fair and just approach, you will be in a strong position to foster resolutions with far more satisfying outcomes.

Reversed

In reverse, *Justice* is a warning of unjust circumstances where the scales are not tipped in your favour. Reframe your approach and take an alternative perspective. You are missing something crucial that helps you secure a fairer result. Take a moment to collect your thoughts and steady your mind before moving forward. Resist the urge to indulge in self-reproach or assign blame; instead, summon your inner strength and take purposeful action. Remaining idle is not an option because inaction leads to stagnation.

By making the conscious choice to grow through authentic and inspired action, you find clarity, allowing you to perceive your own path and the intricate interconnectedness of all lives. It is within this broader perspective that you recognise the inherent wrongness in the subjugation of others, whether based on race, gender, ability, identity, or belief. Such acts reflect a heart and mind in turmoil. A life driven by fear and anger in response to a changing world is a life diminished, yielding only sorrow and unrest. Let compassion be your guide, choose peace over conflict, and embrace the beauty of life, for it is far too fleeting to be spent in the shadows.

Narrative

The Warrior and the Veiled One are forever at each other's side. The gods breathed life into them eons ago to ensure the human world was protected. The Warrior and the Veiled One stand as a unified symbol of choice. When situations calling for justice arise, the Warrior and the Veiled One appear. They offer a choice — fight or embrace peace. If the option is to fight, the might of the Warrior is unleashed, and hell rains down on the world. If peace is chosen, the olive branch is extended. Once accepted, the Warrior and the Veiled One retreat to the divine realm, waiting for their next call.

Correspondences

- » **Astrology:** Libra
- » **Numerology:** 11, 2

Journal Prompts

- » What is the difference between human justice and natural justice?
- » From a holistic perspective, how balanced are you? Are there areas of your life that could use more attention?
- » What is the difference between what is fair and what is right?
- » How important is it to you to be right?

Odin All-Father
XII. THE HANGED MAN

ODIN ALL-FATHER

XII. The Hanged Man

Allow yourself the opportunity for an internal odyssey. A fresh new vision awaits. Adjust your perspective, and the picture will become crystal clear.

In a Reading

A sacrifice will lead to greater wisdom. Surrender grants greater illumination, leading to spiritual evolution. Sacrifices made for the greater good will be well received. This is the unique approach of *The Hanged Man*.

Adjust your worldview and see your situation from a different perspective, giving you a deeper understanding of your circumstances. But you may need to leave your comfort zone to accept this new information. To avoid the cognitive dissonance that arises, stay humble and find a way to incorporate this new viewpoint into your daily life so that you can adjust your thoughts and actions accordingly.

Patience is required at this time, and no amount of action on your part will lead to a swifter outcome. Cutting corners, taking a shortcut, and skipping a step will only slow things down even further, or worse yet, cause you to be stuck in limbo. When you find yourself frustrated, take productive measures to occupy your time. The wisdom you seek will be yours soon enough. Do not rush the process, as this is a sign of a spiritual awakening, and life is about to get a whole lot more interesting for you.

Reversed

The reversal of *The Hanged Man* implies a period of frustration, impatience, and potentially even self-sabotage. Spiritually, it signifies the false prophet and selfishness masquerading as martyrdom. Alternatively, you're engaging in acts of self-sabotage that lead to selfishness. Self-sabotage also leads you to conform to the status quo as a means of fitting in, but at what cost? It's crucial to cultivate patience and self-awareness. Be vigilant against tendencies towards impatience and self-sabotage, and seek a genuine connection to your spiritual journey. Embrace authenticity over conformity, recognising that sacrificing your true self for societal expectations can lead to a hollow sense of belonging.

The contrary nature of this card also signifies that the time of difficult sacrifices is over, and things are moving along. Set yourself clear goals and priorities. Take proactive steps to integrate the lessons learned during this period of sacrifice. Focus on self-care and establish healthy boundaries, allowing your positive actions to be a catalyst for personal growth and fulfilment.

Narrative

According to Norse mythology, Odin hung himself from a branch of Yggdrasil, the World Tree. He pierced himself with his spear and sacrificed one of his eyes, and then peered downward into the darkened waters below. Refusing any aid, he hung there for nine days and nine nights and called to the runes. Eventually, they revealed themselves to him, denoting the acceptance of his sacrifice.

Correspondences

- » **Astrology:** Neptune
- » **Numerology:** 3

Journal Prompts

- » What is surrender?
- » How can you adjust your perspective at this time?
- » What have you sacrificed in the past that has led to further gain?
- » What is your ultimate cure for frustration?

THE FALLEN WARRIOR

XIII. Death

It is a time of transformation, marking an end and a new beginning. You are being guided through the delicate dance and the liberation that comes with embracing change.

IN A READING

When *Death* appears in your reading, it signals a complete transformation, where a matter is brought to a close and a new chapter—or perhaps even an entirely new story—begins. Death is an evolution, and in our lifetime, we may experience many small deaths — times of change and growth, definitive endings that enable an individual to grow and change for the better.

Tie up loose ends and put the finishing touches on things. Completing projects or deciding that you have no more to give will prove to be liberating. Know your limits. Say "no" when you need to, draw boundaries if you must, and be prepared to enforce said boundaries. In some cases, *Death* may highlight that feeling of 'enough is enough'. It encourages you to break habits by identifying patterns that no longer serve your best interests. Such inspired actions can lead to powerful personal transformation and tremendous personal growth. You may even inspire others through your own healing journey.

Reversed

Death reversed is a sign of resistance that manifests as an inability to let go. Dragging out situations and unhealthy attachments could prove destructive. Now is not the time to stubbornly dig in your heels in an attempt to control the situation or bend the will of another. Loosen your grip before it suffocates the very things you are fighting to keep alive. Your period of fear or grieving has gotten out of hand. It is time to address the issue so that healing may take place. Embracing the art of letting go can be the catalyst for a brighter, more liberated future. The contrary appearance of this card brings the promise of liberation and healing. When resistance gives way to release, situations no longer linger in a state of unhealthy attachment. Loosening your grip opens the door to positive transformation, allowing new life to flourish unburdened.

Narrative

Ravens circle the battlefield over the scores of dead bodies lying in ruin. The battle was won but the losses were great, and the time for collecting the dead has come. For one soul, the honour of wings will be bestowed. And so the ravens circle above, in search of the most valiant of the fallen until at last they happen on one — a warrior who held their ground until the bitter end, who stood in defence of family, country, and queen, who had laid down their life for the greater good.

Claimed by the ravens, the spirit of the Fallen Warrior transforms. A new life awaits, one vastly different from the life they knew. The ravens usher their spirit across the veil. There, the spirit of the warrior will be born again, born into a different story with a significantly different ending.

Correspondences

» **Astrology:** Scorpio
» **Numerology:** 4

Journal Prompts

- » What is death?
- » How do you honour a passing?
- » What needs to end in your life?
- » Describe your process of releasing or letting go of something that no longer serves you.
- » Why must things end?

The Hourglass
XIV. TEMPERANCE

THE HOURGLASS

XIV. Temperance

The synthesis of diverse elements and the refinement of one's being guide you through a transformative healing journey.

IN A READING

When *Temperance* appears in your reading, it heralds a time of great external guidance that will assist you in recalibrating and identifying your unique rhythm. Find your sacred balance and the ability to identify and implement harmony in your life. Go with the natural flow instead of trying to control a situation to fit your ideal. Heal through reconciliation, moderate without taking full control, guide instead of govern, and allow yourself to see your situation from various perspectives. These approaches allow for a more rationalised outlook, whereby a state of calm and the much sought-after middle ground is made clear. Harness a more creative problem-solving strategy than what you currently do. Take the tried and true and blend it with an exciting new idea — this may mean accepting outside input. Remember, life does not happen to you. You have the necessary resources in any given moment to effect meaningful change. Temperance is knowing which resources are the most beneficial and in what quantities.

On a practical note, *Temperance* calls on you to get organised. Carefully examine your day-to-day and devise a plan to streamline your approach to tasks. This creates flow and saves precious time. Extend the benefits of organisation to every part of your life, not just work. Take a thoughtful approach to efficiently planning tasks, ensuring time is saved. The results will be a balanced reduction in everyday stresses that rob you of time and peace.

Reversed

Extreme reactions and excessive behaviour left unmoderated will lead to addiction. In reverse, *Temperance* points to erratic or aggressive behaviour. Be mindful of your temper. Regularly and honestly reflect on your actions and their impact on various aspects of your life. Maintaining balance is key to preserving your peace of mind and fostering healthy and meaningful connections with others.

Temperance reversed also calls for a breath of fresh air into a cycle of rigid control. Relax, let your guard and let your hair down for a bit, and enjoy life a little more than you have been. Remember, too much of anything is unhealthy. Loosen the grip and allow yourself the opportunity to go a little wild, take a leap of faith when the occasion calls for it, and seize the bull by the horns.

Narrative

It's life, death, above and below, within and without. It's all and nothing and a combination of each. A timeless tug-of-war that eventually—organically—creates an authentic fusion of ideals and attributes, powers and emotion. In the world of Earthflesh, parents, guardians, heads of nations, and those of divine authority would handpick adolescents of age and send them into the wilderness of the middle world in search of the Hourglass of Life and Death.

After months of braving the elements, one reached it at last. And there on bended knee, without food, water, or aid, the worthy waited for their blessing — a blessing of alchemical knowledge, of an enduring understanding of fusion and synthesis, and the secrets of life and death. Once the blessing had been given, the youth could return to their people, ready to claim sovereignty and henceforth be considered a healer.

Correspondences

» **Astrology:** Sagittarius
» **Numerology:** 5

Journal Prompts

» Describe a time when you have experienced a perfect state of balance.
» Describe a time when your life sorely lacked balance.
» Describe what synergy means to you.
» Describe a time when you felt in a state of harmonious flow.
» Which area in your life do you feel requires healing?
» What does healing mean to you?

THE DEVIL

XV. The Devil

The temptation of instant gratification often leads to bondage, addiction, and superficial pursuits. Be mindful of these tendencies, and remember that the Devil is in the details.

IN A READING

When drawn, *The Devil* signifies liberation and the fast approach of a stroke of brilliance. A time of ecstasy and euphoria may also be indicated, but as with all phases of indulgence, temperance is needed because, as we know, too much of a good thing …

The Devil has an uncanny knack for carnal pleasure and a unique appreciation of the human form. When we lose sight of our physical beauty, it cultivates an insidious lack of self-worth that can, if left unchecked, become quite debilitating. If this is the case, let this card remind you of the wild, unbridled, passionate soul that resides deep in the vessel of your physical form. Have you become far too domesticated for your own good? Find the wild woman or man within you. Act now. Choose ecstatic dance under the full moon. Choose wild nature as opposed to the tame, landscaped outdoors. There is something incredibly primal to be found when we move through rugged, untamed nature, when we climb over tree roots, clamber over rocks, and swim in secluded waterfalls. This card shows you how to connect with Source — the energy binding all life together in a manner that honours the Divine without obsessive attachment and a desire to exploit. Connection to nature in this way will transform your life and the way you perceive all within it.

Reversed

Question your motivations — are you acting out of ego, hidden desires, or what is best and just? The Devil is in the details, and it's in the details that we see the best and worst of people, places, and things. But details are just one part of the grand story. Getting too caught up in them can lead to potentially detrimental situations and the loss of opportunities because of fear and gross dissatisfaction. We risk losing sight of the big picture when we obsess over the details. There may also be an issue of questionable attachments—such as dependency, escapism, and denial—to a person, place, or thing. Take stock of your situation and ask yourself if you are, in fact, submitting to another's will. If so, self-reflection and assertive action are required. By acknowledging and addressing questionable attachments, you gain a deeper understanding of your relationships and behaviours.

Narrative

The Devil is seductive, wily, and lustful in their pursuit of ecstasy. They feed on the wild and excessive. Temptation and the need for euphoric release are their primary objective. The Devil must forever feed to the point where their appetite is satiated. They need you, even if for just a moment. They lure the weak of will, the lost, and the dark of heart to a crossroads, and there demand a decision.

The Devil will appear dressed in fine clothing, boasting a pocket full of enticing promises. Once they have you hooked, you are their plaything. Only then will they reveal their true image — smug and tricksy, they eloquently speak their ultimatums. Their snakes hiss the macabre, seductive, euphoric release of desires fulfilled into their ear. They peer deep into the heart of their prey so they may present fitting temptations — temptations they know cannot be refused. The Devil seeks to bind you to your pleasures, passions, desires … to the deep, dark, ugly places of wild and reckless abandon. Once ensnared, your wishes may be granted — but in return, the Devil will take ownership of your soul. No amount of gold or riches—not even the sacred pearls of Persephone—can release you from your created damnation.

Correspondences

- » **Astrology:** Capricorn
- » **Numerology:** 6

Journal Prompts

- » What binds you?
- » Describe one of your addictions.
- » How do you feel about your body image?
- » Are you asleep to life or awake and embracing it?
- » Describe your ultimate sexual fantasy.

THE MIGHTY OAK

XVI. The Tower

There is potential for newfound freedom amid the collapse of established structures. Focus on establishing strong foundations as you move forward, renewed and wiser.

IN A READING

The Tower signals an unprecedented and abrupt event that may appear destructive, even catastrophic, at first. However, the outcome can potentially be incredibly healing to the soul. Make no mistake, *The Tower* will test you. As situations unravel and bones are laid bare, the crux of the matter will at last be exposed. Only then can it be dealt with once and for all. It brings forth a culmination of shocking circumstances that lead you through a dark night of the soul. And just like that, it may bring about another rather sudden yet liberating series of events.

In some instances, this destructive nature needn't be the harrowing ordeal that some expect it to be. It may be an out-of-the-blue bolt causing you to act suddenly, spurred to rebuild a better, stronger version of what was at risk of collapse. The old no longer serves you, so free yourself from the chains that bind. This sudden disruption isn't personal, so don't fall into a victim mentality at the sight of it — you still have options. Focus your energy on constructing a new phase rather than yet another phase of repair, and establish strong foundations. The onus is on you as the hero of your story, and it is never too late to take charge. *The Tower* manifests in your life as an epiphany that results in tremendous growth when acted upon effectively. There is a liberating, rejuvenating aspect to *The Tower* that is oftentimes lost in the darker elements — it can be a complete shift in consciousness that awakens you to your full potential.

Reversed

The reversed aspect of *The Tower* reveals your stubbornness and refusal to let go of that which binds you. Stop insisting on living amongst the ashes and rubble of your former life in the desperate hope that things will return to how they were. The destruction was a result of a weak or unhealthy foundation. Let go of what once was and seek a better life for yourself. Break the destructive cycles in your life and liberate yourself from your situation, fully embracing the freedom of a new cycle.

Alternatively, the destructive force of the Tower is not quite a catastrophe, at least not in the way you might have anticipated it to be. In some cases, the fallout isn't even a situation that impacts you at all, meaning it is something you observe from a cosy distance. Lastly, it could signify mislaid blame. Thank your lucky stars that you weren't the one caught in the storm, and give gratitude for the life you have. If you observed this collapse in the life of a loved one, be sure to offer your compassion and support. Be the light in the dark to someone who needs it.

Narrative

Amidst the eloquent tapestry of existence, where dreams and the unknown intertwine, the Mighty Oak stands as a sentinel, its vast branches reaching out to touch the realms between worlds. This arboreal titan, born from a modest seed, has grown to be the guardian of portals — an ambassador between the seen and the unseen. Its enduring presence speaks to the grandeur of nature's design, a symbol of rooted strength connecting earth and sky. This bearer of time's wisdom has graced the stage of history as civilisations ebbed and flowed, leaving behind echoes rustling in its leaves like ancient songs. It has sheltered seekers and dreamers, offering refuge beneath its outstretched arms. Its boughs have been a sanctuary for those pursuing truth and the intrepid adventurers of the heart.

But as the cycles of existence continue their ceaseless dance, the Mighty Oak faces an unanticipated trial. The intricate network of roots, once a testament to its enduring foundation, now quivers with the weight of age and change. The colossus that stood firm now stands vulnerable — a stark reminder that even the mightiest can succumb to the erosion of time.

In this twilight hour, the Mighty Oak confronts its own fragility at the crossroads, confronted by choices that resonate far beyond the reach of its shade. And though storms may break and splinter the grand old tree, the endearing spirit of the sentinel, with time, will once again rest its mighty branches amidst the stars and stretch its newly grown roots deep into the heart of the earth.

Correspondences

» **Astrology:** Mars
» **Numerology:** 7

Journal Prompts

» Recall a time when you were unjustly treated; describe the 'Towers' in your life.

» What makes up a strong foundation in your life?

» How do you respond in a crisis?

» When was the last time you felt truly liberated?

Two Eagles
XVII. THE STAR

TWO EAGLES

XVII. The Star

You are being gifted with hope, optimism, and inspiration. Be on the lookout for unexpected help while visionary insights and spiritual guidance foster a sense of peace and calm.

IN A READING

There is a light at the end of a dark tunnel, a glimmer of hope to warm the cockles of your heart and ignite the creative fire that proves to be the answer you seek. Sometimes, we expect the light from the Star to come from someone or something external to us. This is not always the case. In some instances, *The Star* represents the powerful light within, reminding you of the beacon you truly are.

This card also signifies a need for a change of focus. It's time to step back, take a deep breath, and gaze at the stars. There is more to this life, more beauty, more wonder, more enchantment, and more magic out there for you to consider. Immerse yourself in *The Star's* splendid beauty. Take time to stop, breathe, ground, and centre your energy. Hear the radiant whispers of the Universe around you, inspiring you to develop new sight and guiding you through your obstacles. Connect to the universal flow of harmony within all things, and allow yourself to radiate love and hope as you bring light to the darkness inside you.

Reversed

You are losing sight of the forest for the trees, becoming so immersed in your issues that the wise counsel from others is falling on deaf ears. Stubbornness blocks progress, born out of resentment of past disappointments. This manifests as doubt and a lack of faith. Stop hiding your light from the world or bringing hopelessness into the world of another. This may be because of old guilt or the feeling of being lost. Or, you find your persistent negativity or pessimism alienates you and affects your healing process. Step into a mindfulness practice where you challenge yourself to observe the negative as well as the good things in your life. Create a gratitude practice anchored in simplicity, and watch as you smile more often. Breathe deeply and give thanks frequently. Doing so will raise your vibration.

Narrative

A great purging swept the land: fires raged, followed by floods. The landscape was unrecognisable, loved ones gone, and homes destroyed. With the sudden loss of his parents, Two Eagles was thrust into leadership, a role he had always feared. Despite his reluctance, he guided his people to seek higher ground, a gruelling 90-day trek through difficult landscapes. Embracing hope and purpose, he inspired his people to find the strength necessary for the journey.

They began their odyssey through mud, swamp, and rushing waters, fighting off scavengers and enduring physical agony. On the night of the dark moon, Two Eagles, on the edge of despair, sought a sign from the gods. Calling for his eagle under the darkest sky, he felt his hope waning. As he fell to his knees, a warmth emanated from his chest, pulling him to stand. He rose, arms outstretched, shining brighter than any star. The familiar flutter of wings signalled the return of his eagle, a blazing symbol of hope.

Illuminating the landscape, Two Eagles' light guided his people, ending their dark night of the soul. The gods had responded, and the legend of the star of hope was born, a guiding light in their darkest hours.

Correspondences

- » **Astrology:** Aquarius
- » **Numerology:** 8

Journal Prompts

- » Describe a moment in your life where you felt truly hopeful.
- » What is one of your biggest aspirations?
- » Do you believe you take the necessary steps in actively striving for your goals?
- » What does faith mean to you?
- » Explain how and why you prefer to guide or be guided.

Kale
XVIII. THE MOON

KALE

XVIII. The Moon

Embrace your intuition and the power of committing to your inner work. Honour the pull you feel to the realm of magic and mystery.

IN A READING

It's a time of magic, where you will be called to immerse yourself in occult wisdom and walk the path of the mystic. Such a path is as intuitive as it is academic. It demands a sacred pledge and, with it, a sacrifice at a soul level. This is the Moon's way of enticing you to prove your worth, and it's a profoundly sacred exchange between you and the Goddess. *The Moon* makes you aware of the need to work with your unconscious mind to liberate your shadow and heal. Put aside your rational mind and your judgements at this time. The ways of the Moon are not typical and can occasionally be unnervingly bizarre. Nevertheless, you will find freedom of expression in the seemingly uncomfortable.

This card calls for self-expression through intuitive and artistic means. Honour the fantastic and whimsical, which aligns with our childlike imagination and connects us with the powerful—yet simple—concept of play. The Moon encourages you to forge a deeper connection with your intuition. Explore and work with it, allowing such skill to lead you through your situation. Divination practices that function in alignment with the water element will help you.

Reversed

The shadow of *The Moon* indicates a disquieted mind or a mind constantly unnerved due to the magnitude of hidden secrets, causing disturbing dreams. If you have manipulated the situation in an act of avoidance, change and apply a mindful strategy. Doing so brings clarity to your mind and, with it, a sense of peace.

It also suggests that your unconscious shadows are getting the best of you. Hidden wounds preventing you from engaging in authentic interactions are now taking their toll on you. Commit to regular shadow-work practice, which is beneficial for self-acceptance, providing you with a greater opportunity to learn who you truly are and reach a state of wholeness.

Alternatively, *The Moon* reversed points to phobias and irrational fears, leading you to dissociate through compulsive behaviour. List any compulsive tendencies and fears you have that hold you back. If this task is challenging, ask a trusted friend for help. Ask yourself, "Where does this fear/compulsion come from? Where is it rooted?" Getting to the bottom of these questions will take time, but with continued effort, you can heal and grow into a stronger, healthier version of yourself.

Narrative

Kale feels the wild and unbridled call of the Goddess. Powerful and restless, she is claimed. She rises from her bed and sneaks out of her cottage to not disturb a soul. Through the forest, she walks barefoot, over leaf, log, and rock, until she finally reaches the centre of the meadow—her sacred place—and gazes upwards at the Silver Lady in the sky.

Then there's the pull, the force of the Lady reaching down from the heavens to unleash the might of Kale. Her head is thrown back, her back arches, her hair shapeshifts into lunar moths, and a circle of power rises around her. Little does she know that she is not the only one. Others in nameless places look to the Lady and feel the claiming with heart and soul. Such is the life of the moon priestess — never chosen by man, always claimed by the Lady herself. And such a claim is never to be refuted.

Correspondences

- **Astrology:** Cancer
- **Numerology:** 9

Journal Prompts

- Is the Moon sacred to you? Describe your relationship, if any, with the Moon.

- What does 'ritual' mean to you?

- Describe the concept of shadow work in your own words.

- Have you ever been asked to keep a secret? How does secrecy make you feel?

- Do you work better in the late hours of the night? What kinds of activity do you typically enjoy during night time hours?

THE WILD SOLAR DANCE

XIX. The Sun

The Wild Solar Dance
XIX. THE SUN

Embrace a radiant celebration of life, and welcome charisma, happiness, blessed unions, and authentic expressions. Abundance and expansive energy await you.

IN A READING

The Sun lightens even the most foreboding of cards, bringing an exuberant magic that evokes optimism and the bright side of any situation. Your sovereignty leads to a triumphant outcome in most cases. *The Sun* is the happiest card in the tarot and will not be brought down by even the most pessimistic of attitudes. You can see through the darkness of any dilemma so you can take the necessary steps to heal. Your spirit is invigorated to act in a manner that promotes integrity and fosters an awareness of a more harmonious way forward.

This card also encourages you to assume a confident stance and serves as a timely reminder to allow yourself to be seen for your merits. Shine your beautiful light out into the world around you. The time has come to do away with self-doubt and rise to the occasion. Choose to be happy. Make happiness a priority and relish the beauty of simple moments. Laugh, dance, play, and above all else, celebrate the life force in you and all living things. Doing so honours the Sun's essence and brings a great sense of joy into your life. It helps you to focus on the good and allows you to maintain a positive headspace.

Reversed

One of the most beautiful things about *The Sun* is that, even in its reversed position, its meaning remains relatively close to that of its upright. The only difference is that you cannot see the joy the Sun can bring and are often content in wallowing in self-pity. Perhaps illness and fatigue have a hand in this pessimistic outlook. While your attention remains fixated on the issue, the world blossoms all around. When this card appears reversed, it reminds you to open your eyes and look around. There is beauty everywhere. There is always light and joy around you, and you need only be prepared to see it. It is a call to action — it's time to harness your internal fire, to do away with the status quo, and march to the rhythm of a life designed by you. Adopt a new perspective and watch how the mood changes, the heart lifts, and a smile touches the corners of your mouth.

Narrative

At the time of the Summer Solstice, when the days are longer than the nights, the Sun shines its radiant light on all, warming from the inside out. This natural radiance causes an abundant expression that consumes the landscapes and gladdens the winter-weary heart. This is the time of the Wild Solar Dance, a celebration of Sun and Spirit that helps to further awaken the earth. When the drums beat louder, the song becomes more joyous, the feet stamp harder on the damp, green earth, and the movements become more ecstatic. Earth awakens and blesses the land with prosperity and happiness.

Correspondences

- » **Astrology:** The Sun
- » **Numerology:** 1

Journal Prompts

- » Describe your happiest moment.
- » When was the last time you truly danced?
- » Describe a time when you adjusted your perspective and a situation transformed.
- » How do you believe you have been stifling your own light?
- » How do your friends make you feel valued and supported?

SHE WHO IS UNNAMED

XX. Judgement

Judgement calls for introspection and clarity, urging you to trust your inner wisdom and embrace divine inspiration for lasting personal growth and meaningful change.

In a Reading

The time has come to atone for your deeds. The choices you made and the actions you took have led you along the path to where you are now. This card heralds a moment of profound clarity—an awakening of sorts, perhaps even an epiphany—of pure divinity, where you have connected with the ancient druidic principle of *awen*, the pure force of divine inspiration.

Judgement is a message — you have the necessary information to make your own judgement of a situation. There is no longer the need to consult with outside forces; the writing is on the proverbial wall. Pay attention to the way you feel deep inside on a soulful level.

Your surface feelings can mask your true emotions, so dig deep. Initiation into a new phase of being is yet another aspect of this card. Life has taught you many important lessons that now form a powerful well of knowledge inside you. Use your power wisely. Such inner knowing can prove to be a powerful catalyst for lasting change.

Reversed

Heed the call, as hard as it may be. Trust your intuition and rely on your inner knowing. This can be a challenge for many, but when you muster up the courage to do so, you will find a sense of peace and validation that is not easy to come by. *Judgement* reversed warns that what you believe you know could very well be a misrepresentation of the facts. Separate your feelings from the raw facts — it will help you level out your emotional responses to the situation and provide you with a much more constructive head space. Delays leading to eventual success are also possible when *Judgement* is reversed, but only after doubt is effectively eradicated. This allows you to look with clear eyes into the horizon of your future. Then, and only then, can you put fruitful plans into motion.

Prejudice may decide to rear its ugly head. Act with courage, dignity, and self-respect, and you will gain the upper hand. Resist the urge to embrace old coping mechanisms and outdated belief systems. Stand firmly in your power so that if a different perspective is required, you have the courage and flexibility to adjust without compromising your core values. Flexibility helps remove the pressure so you can move forward freely and evolve your current situation with grace and respect for all parties involved, including yourself.

Narrative

On the night of the Winter Solstice, the time of initiation is upon her — she who has sat betwixt, unnamed, unseen, in the sanctity of the forest, tended to only by the daughter of the Moon. Disrobing, her hands are bound behind her back, and her eyes are concealed behind a blindfold. Complete trust is given to her carers as her senses are restricted. She is anointed from feet to crown, brushed with aromatic leaves, and led to a sacred place where the will of the Goddess is felt. There, beneath an ancient weeping willow, the crone stands, sword in hand, ready to hear the vows of the initiate and confer with the gods. It is at this moment, in this place, where every initiate must atone for their deeds. Then, and only then, can she be given her name and rise as a priestess of the arcane.

Correspondences

- **Astrology:** Pluto
- **Numerology:** 2

Journal Prompts

- How do you judge what is right?
- How do you judge what is wrong?
- Describe a time when you were unfairly judged.
- What is your understanding of the Hindu concept of *karma*?
- Do you have good judgement? Describe the role of judgement in your life.
- How have you dealt with prejudice in the past?

THE OAK GUARDIAN

XXI. The World

You have reached the harmonious culmination of purpose and the intricate connectivity of life. All doors of possibility are open to you now — which door will you choose?

IN A READING

Drawing *The World* signals a time of expansion and fulfilment, where wholeness is created, ushering you into the next phase of your life and completing a stage of your soul journey. Goals you have done your best to strive towards are well-grounded and coming to fruition. You will experience a profound sense of satisfaction, so keep up the momentum. It allows you to see further than ever before with fresh eyes. Clarity helps you acknowledge a state of completion that is already in play. The pieces may still be moving, but all is in flow, and success is inevitable. Allow yourself to revel in this happiness for as long as it lasts. Remember to be grateful for those things that give meaning to your life.

The world at large is summoning you, and the archetype of the explorer is causing itchy feet. Whether through physical or virtual means, expansion of your current field of consciousness holds the key to your next adventures. In some instances, you may feel the call to explore your ancestral lineage. Such an undertaking can indeed lead you around the physical world and allow you to immerse yourself in many unique cultural treasures. This card may well be a sign of your spiritual expansion, thus heralding a time to deepen your studies and apply what you are learning. Integrate what you learn in order to transform your accumulated knowledge into wisdom.

Reversed

Abundance and cycles of opportunity may go unnoticed by you. Mindfulness and gratitude are great medicine for those who have lost sight of the simple yet integral blessings in our every moment. When *The World* is reversed, it hints at a struggle to identify your true calling. Touched by a feeling of loneliness or isolation that affects you at a soul level, you may feel detached and adrift. Or, you may feel you lack purpose, constantly searching for deeper meaning. Revert focus back to yourself. Love is a great catalyst for change and the most reliable way to uncover your calling. Identify what you love and genuinely sparks your interest. Go in the direction of your passions, and you will find a splendid, hidden world open to you completely.

You may be negatively impacting the world of another. Your words and attitudes shape your personality and everyone around you. This is never truer than when you are a caregiver. Owning your power is understanding how you communicate with the world around you. Understanding your emotional language and shadows is key to ensuring a nourishing impact on your loved ones and the larger world. There are many ways one can thrive in this world — most of which are not conventional. It is up to you to find your rhythm and break the mould handed to you by a society that prefers the 'one-size-fits-all' model. Find the colour, laughter, and richness of experience that you long for. Grab it with both hands and understand how sacred it is. Don't let go until you feel the time has come to do so.

Narrative

The once-vulnerable Mighty Oak now stands as a testament to resilience and renewal. Its vast branches stretch proudly, reaching out to touch the realms between worlds. Its enduring presence speaks volumes about nature's power to heal and fortify, a symbol of rooted strength connecting earth and sky. Now a repository of time's wisdom and the scars of the past, The Oak Guardian has gracefully emerged from its trials. The cycles of existence have not ceased their dance. Having faced an unanticipated trial, it has transformed into a paragon of strength.

A mystical seeker steps out of the portal, a living embodiment of the potential that lies beyond thresholds once thought insurmountable. Her emergence underscores its role as a guardian of portals, a conduit for the remarkable to enter our realm. The Mighty Oak now embodies a realm of boundless possibilities. It stands as a world overflowing with untapped potential and yet-to-be-explored adventures — a symbol of the interconnected beauty that binds all things, a vibrant and radiant world.

Correspondences

- » **Astrology:** Saturn
- » **Numerology:** 3

Journal Prompts

» Describe your world — what does it look, feel, sound, and taste like?

» How do your passions affect your life?

» What does travel mean to you?

» How do you believe you impact others?

» Describe your ideal life; what gives it meaning?

THE BRUXA

The Bruxa urges daring surrender and authenticity, guiding you through change and self-improvement with divine insight. To benefit from her wisdom, let go of unnecessary patterns, embrace magic, and consider new divination practices or seek help from others.

In a Reading

The Bruxa brings a message of daring surrender. She asks you to shed your ego, strip down to your soul, and dare to be authentic in seeking change. She is a diviner and an advocate for the seeker in times of unassured footing. When you feel the ground falling from beneath you, seek her out, and she will hold your hand through the path of thorns. She holds the map and torch while offering help to those willing to help themselves. She holds the card *Temperance* in her hand, reminding you that self-improvement, empowerment, and reflection take time.

To receive, you must be willing to sacrifice. *The Bruxa* harnesses the energy of the divination tool and taps into the realms of the unseen to bring forth divine guidance.

You, the seeker, are ready to begin learning the practice of divination. Though she is mostly associated with cartomancy, the Bruxa is no stranger to divination through tea leaves, shells, bones, scrying, augury, runes, and many other forms that may be your calling.

Reversed

The Bruxa reversed conveys that you will continue to repeat unnecessary patterns until you are willing to let go. She begs you to open your physical and spiritual eyes to the magic in and around you. Understand that you hold the answers to your questions in your subconscious mind. All you need to do is be brave enough to take the first step. She cannot offer her wisdom if you are not willing to hold out your hand. Reach out to the natural world and tune in to the power of your subtle senses. Doing so welcomes the natural world's unpredictable wildcard energy into your life. Treat this as a sacred gift that can be applied well to construct something beautiful.

This reversed card may also bring a message that your current divination practice may need a change or that you have been attempting to divine for yourself while unable to remain objective. Try something different if what you usually consult is not working, or allow another to read for you at this time. Doing so opens you up to an alternative perspective and a thread of opportunity that may have been hidden from you.

Narrative

The Bruxa is a witch, a mystic, and walker of worlds. She calls out to realms behind the veil — above, below, within, and without. She is in tune with the wild and unpredictable rhythms of the Earth Mother and the sacred realm of spirits. She can bend the elements to her will and persuade the ancestors for assistance in times of struggle. She whispers her magical secrets to the trees and listens to the soft voices of flowing waters. The raven and dragonfly are her friends, and she dances with the flames of the cauldron fire. Spirit flows through every fibre of her mind, body, and spirit. Her flesh of the earth, her bones of sacred stone.

Her space holds gifts from the earth, representing each element on her table. Raw crystals affect the room and charge her tools with their energies. The flames of the candles light the way of self-empowerment. White sage smokes from the bowl, smudged throughout the room with the help of feathers she has collected on her walks, offering cleansing and protection for all who enter. The water behind her is of the natural waterfalls that grace her native lands with their peaceful presence. Herbs of all kinds and uses are interwoven along her shelves between voluminous tomes of occult wisdom. The Bruxa invites you to let her guide you in exploring the answers within your unconscious mind.

Correspondences

- » **Astrology:** Scorpio, Saturn
- » **Numerology:** 23, 5

Journal Prompts

- » What have you been unwilling to surrender that could lead to exponential growth?
- » How do you feel about trusting the Universe or the Divine to guide you to where you need to be?
- » What areas of your life could use a little magic?

Minor Arcana

Kingdom of Swords

The breath of life is one of the sacred building blocks forming the foundation of the World Tree and all that is born of it. Breath flows, moving through all things, giving life, purpose, and inspiration to all things.

In the world of Bonestone, the breath of life is associated with the suit of Swords.

Element:
Air

Polarity:
Masculine

Astrological Signs:
Aquarius, Gemini, Libra

Season:
Spring

Cardinal Direction:
East

Minerals of Resonance:
Clear quartz, fluorite

Botanicals of Resonance:
Rosemary, mint, benzoin, broom, lemongrass, hops, lavender, mistletoe, borage, banya pine resin

QUILL

Ace of Swords

Clarity and the potential to start an intellectually demanding project are at hand. Write your intentions, clear your mind, and reconnect with simple, enriching experiences for lasting inspiration.

IN A READING

The *Ace of Swords* brings a moment of clarity and the potential to begin a project requiring intellectual prowess. Consider this card as a nod to your ambitions and a reminder to harness your leadership skills. It is gifting you with a burst of inspiration that has the potential to become a catalyst for great things.

Now is the time to put pen to paper and write. Using a journal, write your intentions, the story hidden inside you, poetry, or whatever comes to you. Allow the ideas that flood your mind to bleed through the page. The appearance of this card in a reading suggests it is time to cleanse mindfully and with purpose. Clearing your inner and outer landscapes will create space for new, crisp energy to move through your life.

Reversed

Reversed, the *Ace of Swords* highlights a pessimistic attitude caused by a cluttered mind. You may be lacking in inspiration, causing stress and tension. Consider nourishing your mind with experiences that enrich your life force. Digesting good literature, beautiful art, inspiring music, and breathing in fresh air may appear to be simple strategies, but they have a lasting effect on us. Reconnect with simple moments of presence and feel your mind relax.

Narrative

Quill is the keeper of chronicles, the great conveyor of truths and of fallacies. But the mind behind it is the driving force. It is inventive, inspired and, as such, a sacred part of the World Tree. It must first begin as a thought, a seed, a moment of clarity amidst the chaos of life. Those who wield the quill create the history that shapes our perspectives of the world. Great care must be taken to ensure the purity of the mind that drives Quill. Sadly, such care is no longer held in high esteem.

Instead, it is the victor who shapes the narrative, whether right or wrong. One must be as cunning as they are discerning in order to feel the truth hidden between the lines of any tale.

Correspondences

- » **Astrology:** Descendant and/or Point of Libra
- » **Major Arcana:** *I The Magician, XI Justice*

Journal Prompts

- » In what area of your life do you feel the most inspired?
- » What techniques help clear your mind?
- » Do you believe you have strong leadership characteristics? Describe your best leadership skills.
- » Close your eyes and take a deep breath — what is the very first thought that comes to mind? Write it down, draw it if you can. Ask yourself, "Why that thought?"

Tella the Traveller
TWO OF SWORDS

TELLA THE TRAVELLER

Two of Swords

Seek quiet contemplation and grounding practices, especially during critical decision-making. Avoiding issues increases tension, so act with integrity to find resolution and maintain peace of mind.

IN A READING

The *Two of Swords* appears as a sign that you need to enter a phase of quiet contemplation. Meditation and grounding practices prove beneficial to you at this time, particularly if you are in the process of making an important decision. If you should find yourself at odds with situations that appear rife with contradictions, find solace in your inner voice. Your intuition can be a great aid. Never be afraid to connect with it and allow it to guide you. There is tension brewing in the distance. This tension may be something that has been building for some time, yet you cannot reach a point of resolution. Know that continued avoidance of the issue will be counterproductive in the long run. Act with integrity and check in with your moral compass. Doing so will have you acting with authenticity. There can be no regrettable mistakes when you operate from a place of authenticity.

Reversed

The *Two of Swords* reversed is a sign of ongoing dilemmas, a period of mental stress that affects your peace of mind. There is a choice to be made in order to bring about a state of resolution, but you may find yourself stuck between a rock and a hard place. When you find yourself in a place of tension and quarrels, seek out a quiet place to help you think. If it is instead a person causing disruption, distance may help, or a difficult conversation may be in order. Speak your truth with honesty and compassion and work constructively towards a resolution by keeping the channels of communication open and healthy.

Narrative

Tella is a strong-willed mother who lives the life of a nomad. She knows all too well the power of choice and the far-reaching consequences of her decisions. Every choice she makes impacts the child she carries on her back and cements an experience that will shape them both, for better or worse. Tella knows there are times when she cannot trust her own judgements. In times of hunger, when she is road-weary or sleep-deprived, she knows the necessity of reaching beyond to the realm of the Divine. She stops and removes the pendulum from her pouch. This pendulum belonged to her mother, and her mother's mother, and beyond. She plants her feet, steadies her breath, and reaches out with her mind. She need not wait for long. Her practice is refined, and her guidance comes quickly.

Correspondences

- » **Astrology:** Moon in Libra
- » **Major Arcana:** *II The High Priestess*, *XII The Hanged Man*

Journal Prompts

- » What are your best problem-solving strategies?
- » Are you an effective decision-maker?
- » Describe your best decision-making strategies.
- » How often do you rely on your intuition?
- » What is the language of your intuition?

The Charred Heart
THREE OF SWORDS

THE CHARRED HEART

Three of Swords

Sorrow and conflict intertwine, causing inner turmoil and the destruction of love. Yet, from this heartbreak emerges a pathway to breakthrough, understanding, and transformative healing.

IN A READING

When the *Three of Swords* appears in your reading, it may be a confirmation of sorrow. The heart is rife with sadness. It yearns for relief and understanding, and this card can mark a time of acceptance. This acceptance may appear through a flood of tears and the heart-wrenching agony of loss.

But not all is bleak — through the grief of our experiences comes wisdom that lightens the heart.

It brings a clarity of perspective that illuminates a clear path, leading to generative growth. While the memory of great sorrows may linger in your mind, they do not define you. Instead, they teach you the resilience of the human spirit. Life can thrive like never before, thanks to the wildfires in our lives.

Reversed

When the *Three of Swords* appears reversed, it is a sign of denial in dealing with such things as conflict, loss, and sorrow. This lack of acceptance may result from not truly understanding the events that brought you to this place of unhappiness. It's crucial to gently explore the emotions and circumstances that led to this moment. Take some time for self-reflection and view the situation from different perspectives. Journalling or talking with someone you trust can help you fully clarify and process these feelings.

It may also indicate an individual who has allowed their pain to define who they are. They now play the part of the martyr, feigning woes to feed off the sympathy of others. If this is the case, it may be the time to seek professional help. A medical professional may be the right option here.

Narrative

The wild heart burns … charred and defeated, it knows great pain. And yet, pain is not the bringer of death but the catalyst for change. The immensity of pain that touches the heart results in clarity and understanding. The heart will not be defined by its wounds — it will heal, and from those wounds, a great tree will grow. It will tower over the valley, and its branches will arch over the mountains. It will be a source of wisdom, food, water, and wood. It will be a home to those who need one and a shelter in the storms. All will know the story of the oak born out of this charred heart.

Correspondences

- » **Astrology:** Saturn in Libra
- » **Major Arcana:** *III The Empress*, *XIII Death*

Journal Prompts

- » Do you allow your sorrows to define you? Describe the strategies you have in place for dealing with sorrow.
- » What valuable lessons have been born of sorrow?
- » How well do you know sorrow?
- » How well do you heal from physical, emotional, mental, and spiritual wounds?

BATTLE-WORN WARRIOR

Battle-Worn Warrior
FOUR OF SWORDS

Four of Swords

You are being called to rest. Now is not the time for action. Take this moment to unplug and unwind. Rest so that you can approach the next phase of action with renewed purpose.

IN A READING

The *Four of Swords* is a reminder to take a break. If you have been working too hard or have been through a period of stress, rest is long overdue. Respite will bring with it a beneficial new perspective. Utilise this new outlook to give you the upper hand in your endeavours.

One way is to cultivate a fulfilling spiritual practice that brings you peace. Activities that replenish the body, mind, and soul are also recommended. Try yoga, somatic healing, or meditative mindfulness practices. Bring harmony to your physicality by honouring your body with nutritious food and hydrating fluids. Reassess what you eat and drink to ensure you are adequately nourished — this will help your body heal. Be sure you are having enough sleep. When sleep is not possible, meditation may be of benefit. The goal is to calm the mind and lower your cortisol levels so that you can truly relax.

Reversed

In a contrary position, the *Four of Swords* suggests you are burning the candle at both ends. You may be going through a time of continuous and stressful work that is leaving you depleted. If you are a workaholic, take a moment to assess your work–life balance. Perhaps your situation has very little to do with conventional work and more to do with the tasks in your day that monopolise your time and diminish your productivity. Balance is crucial to ensuring a healthy lifestyle. Should you find that you are succumbing to frequent illness, that may well be an indicator of too much work or play and not enough rest.

On the other hand, this reversed card might suggest a pause in your resting period because a situation requires you to assert yourself decisively. Trust your intuition to guide you in choosing the right moment to express yourself. Be compassionate yet focused with your communication to avoid ambiguity. There is peace in knowing where you stand. Be sure to afford that peace to others.

Narrative

The Battle-Worn Warrior carries his wounds on the inside. His muscles ache, his mind remembers the atrocities of war, and his hands have the mark of his swordcraft. The warrior knows how important sanctuary is in his recovery. He knows he will meet his end in the next battle if he cannot find a sanctuary that allows him to recover, remember, and forget. He goes to the blue pool, a place reputed for its healing properties and sacred to his people. There, he lets go and gives his mind the peace it deserves. This small act of self-care brings with it the gift of perspective, which triggers his strategic mind. This is the difference between life and death for this warrior, granting him tremendous confidence in his future battles.

Correspondences

» **Astrology:** Jupiter in Libra
» **Major Arcana:** *IV The Emperor, XIV Temperance*

Journal Prompts

- » When was the last time you fully rested?
- » What does 'sanctuary' mean to you?
- » How do you feel about the practice of meditation?
- » What role does nature have in your healing?
- » Describe your health and wellness journey.

Peanut
FIVE OF SWORDS

PEANUT
Five of Swords

Adversity and disadvantage prevail, creating a feeling of being downtrodden and facing unfair circumstances. Honour your losses and regroup.

IN A READING

The *Five of Swords* signifies unavoidable loss. It could be the loss of a loved one, a health scare, or an unexpected loss in your career or home life. The resulting adversity leaves you at a great disadvantage. The odds are indeed uneven, and it will take a rational mind to disarm the situation. Outsourcing to an expert is called for in order to gain the objective perspective you can't have whilst immersed in this situation. Should you feel that you are at the mercy of your disadvantages, please think again — there is power of will to be found in you. Such an iron will is capable of moving mountains. The human spirit is capable of magnificent accomplishments, even when all the odds are stacked against you. Do not succumb to indolence, addiction, or excessive proclivities. There is no time for a weak and idle mind. It is time to face your fears. Choose to take your power back and work through your afflictions to break yourself free from these mental bondages. No one can do this for you. Start by deciding on an action you can take right now. Go for a walk around the block, send that email, call that person, or make that appointment. Whatever it may be, take action now so that you can build up the momentum required to get the ball rolling again. This is life, so live it.

Reversed

The *Five of Swords* reversed appears when you have lost self-control and your fears—however irrational—have taken a firm hold of you. Detrimental coping mechanisms may be affecting your ability to rationalise your situation. Such an attitude may prove to be the catalyst for both future conflicts and the deterioration of relationships. If you find yourself dealing with issues surrounding abuse, substance addiction, and oppression, please seek out professional help to support you in this challenging period. There is no shame in seeking help when your situation exceeds your capabilities to control. These professionals have plenty of experience and have helped many people with the same problems. You're not alone in this situation; they will help you find a way out. It takes tremendous strength to decide to help yourself — those who do have the heart of a lion.

Narrative

Peanut was the scrawniest kid in his village. He was given the moniker 'Peanut' when he was just three years old. Despite his small size, Peanut had "more heart than a lion", his father would say — and truer words were never spoken. There were no warriors to defend his small rural village when the City of Silver invaded. Peanut lived in an agricultural pocket where there were no warriors nor conflict sufficient to warrant a warrior presence in the village. Fear took hold when the City of Silver and their gleaming soldiers descended upon Peanut's village, and no one would stand in defence. No one except for Peanut. He refused to back down in the face of such tremendous adversity, so they shamed him. They beat him effortlessly in combat, exposing him to public defeat. Peanut may have lost the battle, but his village did not lose the war.

Correspondences

- » **Astrology:** Venus in Aquarius
- » **Major Arcana:** *V The Hierophant, XV The Devil*

Journal Prompts

- » Recall a time when you felt at a disadvantage. What feelings were present? How did you respond?

- » Do you allow fear to hold you back? Describe how you navigate fear.

- » How do you cope in the face of conflict?

- » If a loved one was going through tremendous conflict, how would you support them?

ODESSA

Six of Swords

As you navigate troubled waters, distance brings separation from conflict, yet anxiety lingers. Brace yourself, for success follows the overcoming of troubles.

IN A READING

The *Six of Swords* reminds us that through distance, we can awaken to the beauty of the world once more. Time heals old wounds. Likewise, the separation caused by distance allows us the clarity that is denied when we are in the thick of it. Fresh air brings with it a fresh perspective. A change of scenery can be the right kind of medicine for you. Take a drive or plan a trip. Get yourself out of your familiar surroundings so that you can open yourself up to the energy of something fresh and new. Doing so will stimulate your intellect, and inspiration is sure to follow.

Reversed

The *Six of Swords* reversed signals a time of disrupted travel plans, leading to a period of frustration. You may be unable to get the required distance from what afflicts you now. Take a moment for yourself and engage in a task that helps you to fill your proverbial happy cup, such as going for a walk or reading that book you've meant to finish. Strengthen your boundaries and practise a bit of sacred selfishness. This will help you separate somewhat from your troubles and give you the space to approach them with fresh energy and perspective.

Alternatively, this card reversed can symbolise a disruptive conflict of ideas, leading to an inability to let go and move on. This brings with it negative attachments, confusion, misunderstanding, and mental stagnation that manifest as an inability to focus. Do not let yourself get caught up in ambiguity or confusion. Not every idea is worth holding on to, so be prepared to edit any conflict of ideas while being willing to let go of anything that doesn't flow well. Letting go is key to ensuring that things continue to move forward unencumbered.

Narrative

Odessa knows distance will bring the inner peace she longs for. With only the stars to guide her, she must traverse the rough sea in search of that place that grants her respite from her woes — there is nothing more she can do to resolve her conflict. It is time to disconnect from her situation and seek a life outside of what she knows. The stars do well to guide her, and the sea knows her name. The gods will ensure safe passage until she reaches land again.

Correspondences

» **Astrology:** Mercury in Aquarius
» **Major Arcana:** *VI The Lovers*, *XVI The Tower*

Journal Prompts

» Where would you love to travel?
» When has distance gifted you with a healing perspective?

THE SHADOW EMISSARY

Seven of Swords

The essence of cleverness and cunning prevails, marked by intense communications and the allure of secrecy. Something is being hidden from you or by you.

IN A READING

The *Seven of Swords* urges reflection on individuality, boundaries, and integrity. It represents the independent soul who steps outside societal norms, choosing a unique path. While empowering, this can lead to isolation. The key is balancing self-expression with awareness of social dynamics, creating connections without losing authenticity. Secrets and mysteries are central themes. You may be concealing something, or someone may be withholding information from you. Intrigue and gossip could arise, especially if others take an unwelcome interest in your affairs. Protect yourself by setting clear boundaries and safeguarding sensitive communications. Simple steps, like limiting disclosures, can prevent complications. If tempted to engage in secrecy, pause to consider the consequences. Do your choices serve a higher purpose, or might they cause harm? Reflect on the ethical implications of revealing or withholding truths, always grounding decisions in personal values. Mindfulness and integrity in your actions ensure alignment with your ethics, allowing clarity and peace of mind. Trust your inner compass to navigate complexities and move forward with confidence.

Reversed

The reversed *Seven of Swords* signals the harm of dishonesty, self-sabotage, and unclear communication. This card urges you to confront the truth, whether faced with underhanded actions or self-defeating habits. Avoiding reality only deepens the harm. If self-sabotage is at play, reflect on how you may be undermining yourself and consider seeking support to break the cycle.

This card also highlights frustration with ambiguity or fragmented truths. If you're dealing with confusion or evasiveness, seek clarity. Communicate openly and directly and avoid vague or cryptic messages. If others are withholding, calmly ask for clarification to ease misunderstandings. By embracing honesty and patience, you will navigate these challenges more easily. Clear communication and healthy boundaries lift the weight of secrecy and confusion, leading to smoother relationships and greater peace. Trust that, in time, what seems uncertain will become clear, and through openness, you'll find lasting understanding and resolution.

Narrative

The Shadow Emissary was dispatched in secret under a dark moon in the still of the night. The Emissary travelled far and wide to bring a message to a distant ally. They are careful to keep the scroll out of sight because they know the secrets scratched into that piece of parchment. They volunteer without hesitation to deliver the message, and their chieftain agrees. Their stealth is legendary — some say they are the child of the wind.

Correspondences

- » **Astrology:** Moon in Aquarius
- » **Major Arcana:** *VII The Chariot, XVII The Star*

Journal Prompts

- How do you deal with secrets?
- In what situations do you think white lies can be helpful, and when might they cause more harm than good?
- What role, if any, does gossip have in your life?
- Describe your reactions when you are surprised.
- If you saw a friend's spouse with another in a romantic situation, what would you do?

Bel
EIGHT OF SWORDS

BEL

Eight of Swords

Unlock the power within you by transcending the binds of helplessness. Shift your perspective, and a new pathway will be revealed.

IN A READING

The *Eight of Swords* reminds you that your thoughts make up your reality. Outside forces can influence them: our loved ones, peer groups, culture, geography, etc. Our perceptions of self may be far from accurate, yet they may, in fact, be the ties that bind us. It's time to step out of your own head and seek clarity through the eyes of a trusted friend. Ask the difficult question, "How do you see me?" And act on the information you have gifted with compassion and understanding. Get to know yourself well. What motivates you? Find the answer to these questions and others, dig deep and do the work.

This card also suggests you could be bound by unjust circumstances. If this is the case, clear thinking will lead to new perspectives and opportunities to move forward unencumbered. Leaning in to own your power will prove to be powerful medicine in such a situation. You will find the rewards tremendously fulfilling.

Reversed

The reversed version of the *Eight of Swords* reminds you that the mind is a powerful tool. Put to productive use, it becomes a formidable creator. But the mind can also be used as a weapon. Do not allow your power to be turned against you. It heralds an awakening of your power and a deeper, more honest view of yourself. Powerful self-realisations will prove the catalyst for lasting change, so work at cultivating emotional intelligence. Doing so helps you build resilience, while enhancing interpersonal relationships. You can then overcome any self-limiting beliefs holding you back right now. This isn't easy work, but it is deeply rewarding.

Narrative

Bel is beauty, a rose in her kingdom, a jewel. But she does not see herself as the rose, nor does she acknowledge the many compliments she receives every day. Instead, she remembers the taunts of the children in her youth — the name-calling and the barrage of criticism fed to her every day by her mother. She recalls the suffocating expectations placed upon her at a young age and the obligations … oh, so many obligations! These linger in her mind still, quietly confining her. She feels hollow at times and a child at others. She does not yet understand that there is more to life than what her upbringing taught her. There is more choice, more opportunity, more freedom than she can see. She is bound without necessity, by her own choosing. As she stands by the lake, gazing down at her reflection in the stillness of the water's surface, she sees the child within, bound and broken. In that moment she decides — no more! Such a decision works as a powerful catalyst for change, and just like that, her eyes open to a world she once thought was far out of her reach.

CORRESPONDENCES

» **Astrology:** *Jupiter in Gemini*
» **Major Arcana:** *VIII Strength, XVIII The Moon*

Journal Prompts

- » Have you ever recognised a belief about yourself that didn't originate with you? How did you realise that this belief wasn't truly your own?

- » If you were to speak to your inner child, what would they say to you?

- » What limiting beliefs do you see in the world around you?

- » What does 'owning your power' mean to you?

The Beast
NINE OF SWORDS

THE BEAST

Nine of Swords

Commit to your healing journey in which you prioritise the peace and purpose of a beautiful mind. You are in control, so take action and make that much-needed change.

IN A READING

The *Nine of Swords* represents emotional burdens, stress, and anxiety that rob you of rest and peace. You may feel overwhelmed, plagued by irrational fears, or haunted by past wounds. These anxieties can take a toll on your mental and physical wellbeing, leaving you feeling stuck and weary. This card calls for a compassionate approach to self-care. Establish a routine that nurtures your mind and body, incorporating activities like deep breathing or meditation to quiet your thoughts. Reach out to supportive individuals or professionals for help, as sharing your concerns can lighten the load and ease your emotional burden. If you're grappling with past trauma or cruel experiences, it's time to face them head-on. Speak out, seek healing, and take action to protect your mental health. You have the strength to confront these dark moments and transform them into lessons of resilience and growth. By prioritising self-care, seeking support, and confronting emotional wounds, you will gradually reclaim your peace and clarity, emerging stronger and ready to face the world with renewed courage.

Reversed

The *Nine of Swords* reversed signals the easing of anxiety and fear, bringing clarity and relief after a challenging time. While you may feel lighter, it's important to acknowledge the emotional toll this period has taken. Instead of rushing forward, take time to heal from lingering wounds. Shadow work, such as confronting suppressed emotions and fears, is a powerful tool for this healing. Remember, healing is a journey, not a race. If nightmares or sleep disturbances have affected you, their grip may now be loosening. Take a moment to reflect on the messages these dreams or anxieties may have held. What lessons or patterns have emerged? Approaching these experiences with curiosity can provide valuable insights, helping you understand your emotional landscape more deeply. By gently embracing this phase of recovery, you open the door to peace, clarity, and a renewed sense of hope. Trust that this process will lead you to a place of greater emotional freedom and healing.

Narrative

The Beast personifies fear, a shapeless terror lurking in our minds' darkest corners. It haunts us in moments of vulnerability, creeping closer as night falls and defences weaken. In the deepest recesses of our consciousness, its yellow eyes glimmer with malevolent intent, taunting us with visions of disaster and the unknown. It waits in silence, feeding on our doubts and anxieties, growing stronger with each passing thought. Every whispered worry, every sleepless night, nourishes the Beast, allowing it to swell from a faint echo to a towering, menacing figure. What was once a figment of our imagination becomes all too real, suffocating our peace and mocking our weakness. Its jagged teeth glisten as it leans in closer, its presence overwhelming. And just when it seems poised to strike, we wake up—heart pounding, drenched in sweat—but alive. The Beast retreats, banished back to the shadows, though we know it waits, patient and hungry, ready to return when night falls again.

Correspondences

- **Astrology:** Mars in Gemini
- **Major Arcana:** *IX The Hermit, XIX The Sun*

Journal Prompts

- What kinds of dreams do you typically experience at night?
- What does fear look like to you? Describe a time when you were truly afraid.
- Have you defeated a fear? If so, how?
- What is your ideal method for peaceful sleep?

EARTHFLESH

Ten of Swords

Earthflesh
TEN OF SWORDS

Embrace transformations and new beginnings amidst the chaos and rubble of endings. But beware of unconscious attachments that may be blocking your progress.

IN A READING

The *Ten of Swords* heralds an end to a cycle, the conclusion of a time of pain and suffering — a bad end to a bad situation. Feeling worn out and needing a good rest, you can welcome this ending with relief. Seek solace in the death of your afflictions. Cultivate a strong healing practice, and you will slowly recover to a point where you can find joy again. If it's not the end of a cycle for you, you may find yourself in a state of hysteria with a propensity for overreaction and exaggeration. This is an old coping mechanism and, as such, a bad habit. When you do not deal well with endings, letting go proves rather painful. Nevertheless, letting go allows us to move on, heal, and grow. Focus on the positives in your situation.

They may be difficult to see at this time, but I assure you they are there. If you have made sacrifices to end a bad situation, be very proud of yourself. It is not easy to make sacrifices. It takes great character and strength of will.

Reversed

The reversed *Ten of Swords* depicts a time of relief from long-term suffering or a powerful life change. Perhaps you have recovered from a longstanding illness or received a long-awaited diagnosis that frees your mind of worry. Use this opportunity to take direct and inspired action that, with conscious direction, can help you to shift the trajectory of your life towards a better and brighter future. Feel a rise in power that allows you to take charge of your situation and bring it to a conclusion that benefits all parties. Resolutions to situations that have lingered incomplete are brought to a state of completion, and a new phase of life begins.

Narrative

We all come from the great Tree of Life, and to it, we shall all return. The warrior is dead — all that he was now returns to the land. All that remains is his body, food for the ravens. Soon, his body will become a part of the earth while his spirit takes flight.

Correspondences

- » **Astrology:** Sun in Gemini
- » **Major Arcana:** *X The Wheel of Fortune, XX Judgement*

Journal Prompts

- » How do you cope with endings?
- » When was the last time you sacrificed something in your life?
- » How do you cope with mental pressure?
- » What motivates you to keep going when the going gets tough?

YOUNG MERLIN THE APPRENTICE

Page of Swords

Nourish the mind and satisfy your many curiosities by becoming an eager student with a thirst to learn.

IN A READING

The *Page of Swords* heralds a time of experimentation. Exercising your mental faculties proves to be a wonderful catalyst for learning and growth. This also describes the archetype of the Page's personality (see the following 'As a Person' section). As such, this card signifies a love of writing and journalling that is less emotional and more logical. Honour what your heart and mind have to say, don't hold back, submit to the process, and anchor your thoughts onto the page.

You may find your curiosity piqued by new technologies and foreign concepts, leading you into a space of detachment. Such modern conveniences will undoubtedly ignite the inner child and bring a sparkle to the eye. Now is a good time to research and clarify your thoughts and feelings about a subject. The more information you have to work with, the clearer your understanding of that subject will be. Only then can you confirm if your curiosity is indeed warranted or if it was simply born out of benign ignorance. Sometimes, taking a few steps back assists you in gaining a greater perspective of your situation. Be sure to prioritise technologies geared towards learning and growth. The mind is a hungry thing, so be sure to feed it good food.

As a Person

As a person, the Page is young at heart and curious, with a natural aptitude for learning and an inquisitive mind. He is articulate and quick-thinking, making him rather responsive. He makes for a wonderful academic writer and thinker, and he needs to know how things work.

This Page is also quite intuitive. Perhaps this is how his mind can move so swiftly — part of it is connected to a higher source of inspiration that helps him analyse, calculate, and act with rapid speed.

Reversed

The *Page of Swords* reversed depicts the petulant child. Insubordination is likely, as they fancy themselves as an expert after reading just a few chapters of a book and knowing next to nothing. Their youthful arrogance leads them to confuse enthusiasm with expertise.

This card is a reminder to relax a little. Now is not the time to seek control of a situation. More information has yet to be learned. You may also find that your mind is moving too fast and that you are constantly 'on'. Meditation may help to quieten the mind, thus placing you in a state of relaxation. The quieter the mind, the more peace you invite into your life. Sleep will be vastly improved, as too will productivity and focus. A calm and tranquil mind also helps you clarify your needs and any blockages or resistance you have towards your goals.

Narrative

Young Merlin practised his skill as a wizard's apprentice. He was dedicated, gifted, and methodical. His curiosity oftentimes got the better of him, and he ended up in situations that resembled chaos. This is why his teacher moved him from the king's castle to a cave. There, he would be free to conjure to his heart's content, and the good townspeople would be none the wiser. Or so they thought. Young Merlin had quite the gift, particularly when it came to the air element. Each time he conjured even a fraction of his power element, all within his cave would spring to life. The rock walls that sheltered him would simply disappear.

Correspondences

» **Astrology:** Libra
» **Elemental Combination:** Earth of Air

Journal Prompts

» Describe what the *Page of Swords* looks like to you.
» When you think of Merlin, how do you feel?
» Do you have a love for learning? Do you enjoy writing? If so, what type of writing do you enjoy?

ATHENA

Knight of Swords

Athena
KNIGHT OF SWORDS

Embrace courage and wisdom as you move forward on your path. Focus on strategy to help you devise a winning plan to achieve your goals fearlessly.

IN A READING

When the *Knight of Swords* appears in your reading, it suggests that championing a cause is in order. What causes do you feel most passionate about that you could make a swift and positive change to? Employ strategic thinking to gain the upper hand in your situation. You may feel a surge of innovation. When applied effectively, this leads to successful undertakings.

Courage is yet another aspect of this card. You demonstrate a certain level of mastery over your thoughts. The brave-of-heart face their challenges despite their fears. This card challenges you to face your fears and take action where you've been reticent. Your courage may resemble daring, depending on your approach, but don't worry about how others may perceive you. Your courageous actions prove advantageous in mentally disarming any opposition, and you will succeed where you previously did not.

As a Person

As a person, the Knight of Swords signifies an individual possessing a valiant heart and whose courage is the very light that illuminates. This Knight is a quick thinker, decisive, and a champion for justice. The wisdom she possesses is part of a larger arsenal. Headstrong and deliberate, she runs into the fray, eager to intellectually dominate. This attitude demonstrates her arrogant side. Nevertheless, there is an inherent nobility to this character that commands a certain level of respect and perhaps even trust.

Reversed

When the *Knight of Swords* appears reversed, it is a sign that you are acting on wild instinct rather than intellect — a cavalier attitude, more concerned with winning and being right than resolving the situation. It can highlight the rot festering in those once pure of heart. This rot can result in the rampant corruption of ideals, igniting tempers and quarrels.

The reversed card also represents an individual who does not stop to think before they speak. This lack of a verbal filter negatively impacts those around them, leading to unnecessary misunderstandings and hostilities. You may need to work a little harder to be able to breathe a little kindness into your communication style. But doing so will endear people to your cause. Alternatively, the reversed card depicts a brilliant mind that has become idle over time, leading to dissatisfaction and questioning one's worth. It's time to focus on feeding the idle mind. Learn a new language, pick up a new skill, increase your knowledge on a subject that interests you or impacts your life or the life of a loved one. Kickstart a good mental flow and watch as inspiration slowly but surely comes running back to you.

Narrative

Lethal, she rides, sword in hand, across the valley to meet with her war party. She has been formulating a brilliant battle strategy as she rides. The owl by her side is ever watchful, feeding her the jewels that will be her crowning glory. This plan, above all others, will cement her name in history. This battle will define her, and from it, a mighty legend will arise.

Correspondences

- **Astrology:** Gemini
- **Elemental Combination:** Air of Air

Journal Prompts

- Do you believe in chivalry? Is the concept of chivalry something that you feel you understand?
- When did you last feel courage?
- If you could champion a cause, what would it be?
- Write down one piece of earned wisdom.

THE MORRIGAN

Queen of Swords

Acknowledge and honour the expertise and passion that you cultivated in your life. Someone may very well be in need of your particular brand of innovation.

IN A READING

When the *Queen of Swords* appears in a reading, the time for diplomacy is upon you. Use your peacekeeping qualities to soothe situations and be perceptive above all else. Cultivate an eye for detail and bring your indomitable spirit forth into action. Tact and diplomacy will only get you so far — persistence will get you across the line.

Be artful with your communication, and hone the power of the wordsmith. People are drawn to you for your clarity of thought and rational thinking. The Queen of the air element is fair and just, and such qualities often indicate a trustworthy confidante. You are a vault to those who wish to unburden their conscience, as well as those who seek out a differing perspective. It's important, however, for you to determine if you are able to carry the mantle of confidante before accepting such a responsibility. Prioritising your boundaries can help greatly in this instance.

As a Person

The sword-wielding Queen embodies someone with a dignified presence and a sharp eye for detail. Articulate and clever, she listens actively and responds thoughtfully, making others feel heard. She values truth, even when it's brutally honest, though any hurt caused is unintentional. Her forthright nature can seem insensitive at times, but her love for deep questions and wide-ranging interests—especially literature—make her a natural-born teacher and occasional writer. She knows how to charm when needed. In her reversed form, she may represent someone struggling with loneliness, whether as a divorcee, widow, or someone unfulfilled in their singlehood. She can also show challenges in relationships, where her critical nature may cause misunderstandings. At times, she might be overly protective of her emotions, leading to communication that feels sharp or defensive.

Reversed

The *Queen of Swords* reversed signals confusion and ineffective communication, often stemming from hidden emotional pressures or unresolved issues. Reflect on your motivations and identify any triggers affecting your thoughts or interactions. This self-awareness can help you gain clarity and relieve some of your mental strain. You may find yourself in a relationship where you or another person is overly controlling or smothering with too much unsolicited advice or criticism. This dynamic can breed co-dependence, hindering personal growth. Recognise these patterns and allow space for each other to thrive. Understanding your attachment style can provide insight into your emotional needs and improve your interactions. Alternatively, you may be dealing with an enabler who makes things easier but fosters reliance. While convenient, this can cause long-term coping issues. Cultivate healthier strategies for dealing with stress, such as journalling, exercising, or spending time outdoors. By relying on these tools, you'll shift from a reactive to a proactive mindset, helping you navigate challenges with resilience and clarity. This card reminds you that through introspection and healthier boundaries, you can regain balance and move forward with purpose.

Narrative

The Morrigan holds a formidable legend. Ravens are kindred to her, and so too are crows. Her legacy is that of battle and war. She is sovereign and will bring sovereignty out of those she deems worthy. Although a great teacher, her lessons are less than conventional. She will push you further than anyone before. You will feel the pressure, and you may even crack. But one thing is certain — once she is done with you, your life will never be the same. The cult of the Morrigan is indeed real. Fathers and mothers send their daughters to her to be 'made'. The child will later emerge as a warrior of the old ways, skilled in both the art of battle and sorcery. The daughters of the Morrigan are feared and respected across the land. Even the dead know of them.

Correspondences

- » **Astrology:** Libra
- » **Elemental Combination:** Water of Air

Journal Prompts

- » How often do people seek your advice, and what kinds of guidance do they usually ask for?

- » How would you describe your communication style, particularly when conveying important information?
- » What aspects of teaching do you find most fulfilling or challenging?
- » How do you feel about the dynamics of your current relationship, and what aspects contribute to its health or wellbeing?

King Arthur
KING OF SWORDS

KING ARTHUR

King of Swords

A leader with a noble heart and a sharp mind can prove invaluable to your cause. This is a good thing, too, as you may need an expert decision-maker.

IN A READING

The *King of Swords* signifies a time for hard and fast decision-making. Your wit and sharpness of mind prove to be quite handy in a bind. You are coming into your own and tapping into a fountain of wisdom that will aid you in your endeavours. You have a natural aptitude for being a teacher of profound topics such as philosophy, spirituality, and the occult. Be prepared to tap into the wise elder within you and provide the necessary support to the people around you. Or you are called on to parent — either literally or figuratively. By following the natural inclination to serve your community, you find yourself in a position of governance that suits you perfectly. But with great power comes great responsibility. Now is not the time to rest on your laurels but to be a champion for the people relying on you for much needed and long-lasting change. Be kind to others during this time, as you never know the struggles others have faced in their lives. Being gentle and curious will go a long way in helping others restore their faith in the human race. Honouring this mantle of responsibility isn't easy, but is greatly rewarding.

As a Person

As a person, this King represents a natural leader. Even when he doesn't try, others will stop and listen and follow his instructions to the letter. He is a fantastic decision-maker, finding the task easy because he knows that decisions are a part of everyday life — they are not personal. He has a fatherly, wise-man grace, a way that makes him trustworthy. He is a wonderful listener and a strong counsellor — an honest person motivated by the truth in all things.

Reversed

When the *King of Swords* appears reversed, it points to a lack of clarity and integrity in your interactions with others and within yourself. You may encounter people who are self-serving, manipulative, or unwilling to take responsibility for their actions. They may try to exploit you or cause confusion, leading you to question what is true. Alternatively, you might be caught in daydreaming or indecision, unable to follow through on your goals. Protect your boundaries and trust your instincts. Be cautious about who you allow into your inner circle, and be mindful of any feelings of doubt or confusion. Stay grounded and avoid getting lost in illusions or distractions. Taking clear, responsible action and being honest with yourself will help you navigate any challenges, allowing you to regain clarity and move forward with confidence. By staying true to your values and keeping your focus sharp, you can avoid manipulation and regain control of your situation. Embrace this opportunity to strengthen your discernment and trust that your clear, responsible choices will lead you to a future filled with authenticity and self-assurance.

Narrative

Arthur was a great king whose rule over his kingdom was legendary. Loved by his people, he ruled with dignity and nobility. The kingdom thrived under his rule in all areas, from agriculture to the arts. He was kind and gentle with others. His people looked up to him for wisdom.

But Arthur was not always a king, and the trials and tribulations that shaped his legacy were indeed great. Perhaps this is what made him so humble. He was not born with a crown on his head — it was given to him by the people. Arthur was a chosen leader and a beloved one at that.

Correspondences

- » **Astrology:** Gemini, Aquarius
- » **Elemental Combination:** Fire of Air

Journal Prompts

- » If you were to speak to the wisest of elders, what would they say to you?
- » What is your relationship with your father like?
- » What natural leadership talents do you possess?
- » Are you a fair and gentle communicator? Describe your communication style.
- » Is being truthful important to you? How do you strive for truth?

Minor Arcana

Kingdom of Cups

Womb water is the lifeblood that courses through the veins of the World Tree. It is what nourishes its ancient roots and breathes lifeforce and spirit through every part of it, from leaf to root. Womb water is the conduit of the Divine, the maker of life as we know it. It activates the senses, helping us feel our way through life with a gentle flow that connects to a harmonious existence.

In the Bonestone, womb water is represented by the suit of Cups.

Element:
Water

Polarity:
Feminine

Astrological Signs:
Cancer, Scorpio, Pisces

Season:
Autumn

Cardinal Direction:
West

Minerals of Resonance:
Cowrie, labradorite, halite, enhydro quartz, pearl, moonstone, neptunite, opal, coral

Botanicals of Resonance:
Adam and Eve Root, African violet, maidenhair, chamomile, apple, belladonna, jasmine, lotus, vanilla, yarrow, lucky hand

THE SUPER BLOOD MOON ECLIPSE

Ace of Cups

The Super Blood Moon Eclipse
ACE OF CUPS

It's time to open your heart to the overpouring of love and joy into your life. An unexpected blessing awaits you.

IN A READING

The *Ace of Cups* suggests a new romantic connection is about to be made, affections declared, or intentions set, resulting in a heart bursting with joy — a 'cup runneth over' flavour, so to speak. This is a phase of pure happiness and resplendent beauty. Immersing yourself in the experience is the best action to take, reciprocating with positive affirmations that acknowledge and honour the feeling. Pay it forward and take conscious and inspired actions that lead you towards greater blessings and positive change. Demonstrating gratitude aligns the heart with abundance and keeps you in a flow state.

Setting intentions keeps you aligned with your goals and harnesses the power of focus. We are what we choose to focus on. The *Ace of Cups* is the perfect reminder to keep a healthy intention-setting practice, perhaps once a month on the new moon.

This card also signifies the creative and life-giving power of the womb. You may find yourself in a state of emotional and creative fullness, a physical or psycho-spiritual pregnancy or birth. Take advantage of your ignited intuition and embrace your desire to create with aligned action. Honour your imagination however it feels right for you. Allow the fusion of your imagination with your emotional body and create something soulfully beautiful. If this card points to a physical pregnancy, then this child will be quite empathic, caring, and emotional. Connecting with the womb is a powerful journey; whether you choose to connect with your own or another's, you will find a world of creative power available to you.

Reversed

The reversed *Ace of Cups* signals emotional blockages and disconnection, asking you to address areas where your heart feels heavy or closed off. This may stem from past wounds, such as a negative birth experience that left you feeling ungrounded, unfulfilled relationships that no longer meet your emotional needs, or loneliness linked to unresolved ties that prevent you from embracing new connections. Each challenge is a call to heal and renew your emotional wellbeing.

To move forward, focus on practices that restore balance and vitality. Journalling can help you process emotions, while meditation fosters clarity and calm. Rituals like cord-cutting or soul retrieval allow you to release energetic ties that weigh you down. If your relationship feels unbalanced, approach your partner honestly and respectfully to explore healing together. Should they be unwilling, trust your inner wisdom to make the best decision for your future, even if it means letting go. Honour your emotional needs through self-care: spend time in nature, engage in creative pursuits, or reconnect with loved ones who lift your spirit. By embracing healing, you free yourself to experience life's beauty and abundance with a renewed sense of purpose. Trust the process — you deserve joy, love, and fulfilment.

Narrative

When a lunar eclipse occurs close enough to the earth to make it a 'super' full moon, the moon turns blood-red—the colour of creation—and bleeds its creative energy into the waters of the world. Such an event is sacred. Witches, druids, and mystics of the world gather by the water's edge in an act of ritual to listen. It is said that along with ancient wisdom, the narratives of our ancestors are heard, granting each of us strength. A new phase begins once the ritual is complete, and the waters of the world are once again holy.

Correspondences

- **Astrology:** *Imum Coeli* or 'bottom of the sky' (IC)
- **Major Arcana:** *I The Magician, XI Justice*

Journal Prompts

- Describe a purely happy moment in your life.
- Write down three things that you are grateful for.
- What is your favourite 'meet-cute' — a charming or unexpected first meeting between two people?
- What is your relationship with the womb?

Kindred Spirits
TWO OF CUPS

KINDRED SPIRITS

Two of Cups

We heal to be whole, and when we are whole, we can fully connect to one another with body, mind, and spirit. Love and genuine connection are then possible.

IN A READING

The *Two of Cups* signifies a kindred spirit entering your life, which has a transformative effect on your heart — it blossoms, opening to the world so it can receive. Such a connection is founded on mutual respect. The establishment of a shared relationship language begins to take place.

A new phase of sensual expression, beauty, and pleasure also unfolds. This results in a phase of creativity and an immersion into beauty that truly nourishes the soul. Or you may find it has a positive effect on your health from a holistic perspective. Whichever the case, the arrival of this card heralds harmony and creativity through a union of opposites. Opposites indeed attract — likewise, our counterpoints can help us to complete creative projects. Opening up to a partnership like this proves mutually beneficial.

Reversed

The reversed *Two of Cups* suggests a relationship has soured, and no one stands to benefit from it in its current form — discord and breakdowns in communication increase, as well as a sense of loneliness. You may experience this as broken promises, unreliability, or a lack of trust. What usually happens is that old wounds from previous relationships start to ache once more. You may find yourself repeating a cycle where past events are once again affecting you. Acknowledging the cycle and learning how to break free of it is your lesson in these moments. Jealousy and possessiveness are diseases that eat away at your relationships until they lie in bitter ruin. Know when it is time to walk away — don't wait for it all to go down in flames.

Counselling and therapy will be of tremendous benefit to you (and your partner) and help you break free of these negative cycles in your life. So too would shadow work, as it dives deeper into your unconscious mind where things stay hidden. Commit to doing the work and watch how fast patterns emerge and change. Know yourself, take back your power, and cut cords where necessary. And when you do, you will have freed yourself to move forward with a newfound respect for yourself and a deep reverence for the wisdom you have learned.

Narrative

The meeting of a kindred spirit is one of the most sacred of unions. Such a relationship, such a soul connection, transforms the heart and the mind and unifies each in a state of pure love. To find a kindred spirit is a rite of passage. Men and women of age are sent on a pilgrimage to explore all the nations of the earth. Such a pilgrimage will take them far. They traverse mountains, sail over water, and cross deserts, all while braving the elements. These youths only find home again when they meet and recognise each other. They wander the earth open, ready to receive.

Correspondences

- » **Astrology:** Venus in Cancer
- » **Major Arcana:** *II The High Priestess*, *XII The Hanged Man*

Journal Prompts

- » What does the term 'kindred spirit' mean to you?
- » Describe your thoughts about soul mates, kindred spirits, and twin flames.
- » Describe your perfect relationship — what are you like in a relationship?
- » What is your definition of an unhealthy relationship?

Cauldron Sisters
THREE OF CUPS

CAULDRON SISTERS

Three of Cups

Embrace the joy of conscious connection with kindred spirits. Come together to make inspired magic through laughter and joy.

IN A READING

You have found your people, your community — a place where you feel you fit in, a group of kind-hearted people with compatible interests. This is the message of the *Three of Cups*. It also suggests a celebration with great company. Joy, merriment, laughter, and libations are around the corner. Let your hair down a little and enjoy yourself, particularly if you have been a bit withdrawn from the social scene. This is the gift of meaningful exchanges. A phase of open and honest interactions can lead to the expansion of ideas through collaborative means, and a meaningful project may begin to take shape. Now is a time to recognise the blessings in your life. A deep sense of gratitude brings a sense of wholeness and belonging into your life. Engagement in spiritual rituals and experiences in group settings—such as moon circles, open pagan circles, covens, and groves—will benefit you and your sense of community and belonging. This is the most important thing for you right now, as it will help you feel connected with yourself as much as with others around you, and that will benefit you in being part of something bigger than yourself.

Reversed

Contrary to the *Three of Cups'* meaning of conscious connection, the reversed meaning signifies someone desiring to withdraw from social groups due to insecurities and oversensitivity. It could also suggest a lack of cooperation and conflict in a group that could lead to its eventual dismantling. There may be a fight for leadership where there is no need for a leader. The ego and dominance of another may be the very crux of the issue. There may be ulterior motives at play, suggesting that the company you keep does not have your best interests in mind. Trust will be broken, and friendships may end. In any of these situations, it's important to understand that not every situation can be saved, so processing your emotions and reaching for healthy coping mechanisms is what you need now. A gentle conversation could prove quite healing; just remember to choose your words carefully. Focus on healthy communication and the cultivation of strong facts. Transparency and a clear objective help dismantle delusions of grandeur. When you feel ready, take steps to honour such endings appropriately. Take solace in removing yourself from toxic situations. Endings can elicit deep feelings of hurt and could lead to isolation and loneliness, so be patient with yourself and move through your emotions with kindness and respect. Use this experience as an opportunity to invest in yourself.

Narrative

The Cauldron Sisters are a force to be reckoned with. They gather for every full moon, every sabbath, every major astrological event to work their cauldron of creation. They laugh, they sing, they hug, and they cry. Together, they create the most magical of elixirs. Their magic infuses the unified tribes with blessings and purpose. Their work stabilises the land's energy and keeps the people's hearts and minds open. Their magic is integral to the harmony of the land. To cross even one of the Cauldron Sisters is to relinquish all that is good in your life.

Correspondences

» **Astrology:** Mercury in Cancer
» **Major Arcana:** *III The Empress*, *XIII Death*

Journal Prompts

» What does the word 'tribe' mean to you in modern terms?
» Describe your role in your community.
» In what situations would you classify yourself as an introvert or an extrovert?
» Describe how you feel when you find yourself alone. Are you solo often?

KEANU THE FISHERMAN

Four of Cups

Boredom brings stagnation and laziness. Add an injection of vitality and gratitude into your life. Inspired action helps break the monotony and refresh the senses.

IN A READING

With the *Four of Cups*, you have reached a point where you feel you have enough, yet long for something more or different. This may appear like ungratefulness, but a lack of gratitude does not stand at the heart of this mild affliction. It is a desire to change pace and try something new without discarding what is tried. It depicts a state of ease, where very little effort is needed to sustain something or daydream. Your projects have reached a point of self-sufficiency, so set your sights on either expanding or diversifying. Allow your mind to rest. Immerse yourself in fantasy or read a great book so you can enjoy the imagination of another. Creative journalling might also spark an interest. As you embrace these imaginative pursuits, potential benefits arise. Through this respite, fresh perspectives and ideas appear to you, enriching creativity and productivity that can be channelled into existing and future projects.

Reversed

You have a restlessness that grips you in a state of wanting. The *Four of Cups* reversed suggests you are dissatisfied with your lot in life, even if you have more than others. Perhaps you are approaching your endeavours with a lazy attitude while expecting you'll be handsomely compensated — and maybe even getting upset when you are not. Reassess your priorities and take stock of your values — do they align with one another? If not, then you need to make important changes. Apathy and self-diagnosed mediocrity manifest as a desire to indulge in substances that alter your state of mind. Be very careful, as the excess of the unnecessary leads you down a very dark path. Work on your concept of self-worth through healthy coping mechanisms and reap the rewards from investing in your own healing journey.

This reversed card also signifies stagnation in your projects, where continuing would be futile. You feel overworked and underappreciated but emotionally obligated to do the right thing. It is time to let go and seek a new endeavour where you will be duly compensated for your time and efforts. When this happens, you'll notice how you feel more energised by your work and grateful and inspired again.

Narrative

Keanu was a fisherman his whole life. He cast his first net at the tender age of two with the gentle guidance of his father, and his skills as a fisherman were nurtured every day after that. His father took pleasure in passing on the secrets of his forefathers, learning the history and myth of his people through the ocean. He knew that by learning to fish, he would always be safe, for he would always have food in his belly. He loved to fish, and he loved spending time with his father, laughing and learning. But times changed, and when Keanu reached adulthood, his interest in fishing waned, and he yearned for other things. He wanted more, so he explored different avenues with his family's blessing and his father's mild disappointment. He cultivated other skills, but no matter where he went and what he did, he always found himself in a boat, on the water, far from land, experiencing the plenty that he once took for granted.

Correspondences

- » **Astrology:** Moon in Cancer
- » **Major Arcana:** *IV The Emperor, XIV Temperance*

Journal Prompts

- » How often do you feel you are bored?
- » When have you felt a sense of completion from an emotional perspective?
- » Were you ever groomed to be something you had very little interest in?
- » Where in your life do you hold back?

THE ELEPHANT WHO MOURNS

Five of Cups

Amidst trials of loss, sadness, and treachery, you are destined to uncover the truth. Only then can you evolve, through change and your shadow self, to emerge triumphant.

IN A READING

A period of sorrow is upon you. You feel you have a genuinely heavy heart, and adversity has gotten the better of you. The *Five of Cups* suggests that your shadow self is more likely to be triggered if you avoid your issues. During this phase of disappointment, heavy emotions weigh you down, so it's best not to make big decisions. Alternatively, you may find yourself unmotivated to deal with your disappointments, simply wishing to be left in peace. However, when your adversities exceed your capacity to deal with them, it is time to ask for help. Seeking help from an appropriately qualified source helps you to gain much-needed perspective, which is important because it enables a deeper understanding of the situation while fostering empathy and open-mindedness.

When old wounds are ignored they linger and shape our lives. Shadow work is the practice of acknowledging and integrating our hidden, often undesirable aspects, fostering self-awareness and authenticity. By confronting these 'shadows', we build emotional resilience and a more balanced sense of self. This process often involves introspection, journalling, therapy, dream analysis, and mindfulness. As time ticks on and the tears lessen, hope will blossom in your core, and the world will look a little brighter. Before long, sadness will be replaced by joy, and the little pieces of your soul you lost along the way will begin to return, once again experiencing a sense of wholeness.

Reversed

A season of sorrow ends, and the heavy heart plaguing you begins to lift. This is a breath of fresh air after a time of despondency. The need to stretch out your heart is a positive sign. A broken relationship is on the mend, and a healing phase has already begun. Doubt is being abolished, and a sense of security is solidly in place. When the *Five of Cups* appears reversed, set your sights on new horizons. Too long have you lain in wait. Now is the time to embrace your opportunity and pursue your curiosities. Because when you do, a whole new world opens up — and that is when the adventure really begins.

Narrative

The Valley of Ivory is a haunted place. There, you will meet with a legacy of cruelty and destruction against the gentle giants of this world. Cruelty is oftentimes employed in the pursuit of luxury. This truth is apparent in the Valley of Ivory. The Elephant Who Mourns comes here every year. They come to remember, to understand ... to seek out peace and shift a heavy heart. Every year, the Elephant chips away at their shadow until, one day, it no longer has a hold.

Correspondences

- » **Astrology:** Mars in Scorpio
- » **Major Arcana:** *V The Hierophant, XV The Devil*

Journal Prompts

- » When have you mourned?
- » Describe a time when you were genuinely sad.
- » How often and how easily do you have a good cry?
- » What do you know and understand about shadow work?

THE FARMER AND HIS WIFE

Six of Cups

Let creative richness be your remembrance and virtue your beauty. Nurture your mind, body, and spirit, finding equilibrium and, through it, reconciliation with your authentic self.

In a Reading

The *Six of Cups* signifies a period of deep nostalgia — there is something beautiful in remembering. When we remember, we honour the past and the loved ones who were integral to it. Right now, fragments of your past are being well utilised. The lessons you have learned, and the sorrows you have dealt with now assist you in achieving success. In this phase of bliss, immerse yourself in emotional and sensual pleasures and make life beautiful.

Feel free to express your sensual nature without fear or guilt so you can nourish your parched soul, bringing you closer to a state of wholeness and fulfilment.

Be generous with your affection towards others. Consider this an opportunity to pay it forward. It costs nothing to be kind and give kindness to others, but the rewards for making such a decision are indeed endless in nature. This card also points to a new family cycle, such as a new addition to your family or a rite of passage for a family member. Our families tend to go through many cycles. It is indeed a privilege to be there to observe the cycles.

Reversed

Events from your past are still playing out in your present — and likely your future as well, unless you break the pattern. This situation manifests as a behavioural cycle keeping you bound to a state of mind where you feel unable to progress. You may feel you have a fresh perspective, revealing things you were previously oblivious to. Take a more honest look at your family and close relationships. It is time to do away with old rituals, old habits, and old ways of being and it's time to create new ones. Change, in this case, is a good thing. Even the smallest changes are beneficial to your situation, such as adding a simple, nourishing ritual to your daily life, like chanting a mantra or short-form journalling. Develop a hobby that serves your mind, body, and spirit. And remember, with change comes growth and wisdom.

Narrative

The farmer visits his wife's grave daily, bringing a posy of forget-me-nots as a symbolic gesture of his enduring affection. Although time may have aged him, and the land he toils has slowly depleted, he still comes every day. The love in his heart for his wife will never fade. She was everything. Now that he is left alone in this world, he lives every day in a state of nostalgia.

Correspondences

- » **Astrology:** Sun in Scorpio
- » **Major Arcana:** *VI The Lovers*, *XVI The Tower*

Journal Prompts

- » Describe a delicious childhood memory.
- » Describe moments when you have felt nostalgic.
- » What is your relationship with family traditions?
- » Describe a time when you felt truly blissful.

THE CHARLATAN

Seven of Cups

Beware the allure of superficiality and indulgence, for they lead to loss. Reach beyond illusion and temptation and beware of wishful thinking where delusions of grandeur take centre stage.

IN A READING

The *Seven of Cups* indicates hoarding — acquiring more than you need. You are running out of physical and mental space to store these belongings. It creates stagnation and a lack of flow. Perhaps you have started to attach memory and sentimentality to the objects in your life, and getting rid of these objects is proving emotionally tricky. No single object holds the memory of an individual or an experience that we have cherished; these are always with us in our hearts and minds. This is a metaphor for having too many choices, each more enticing than the last. Choose those things that add value to your life. Choose quality over quantity, choose to upcycle, choose to repurpose, choose to donate. You need assistance to clear your head and gain some perspective. Beware of illusions. Ensure you read the fine print carefully so you know exactly what you are committing to when entering into a contract or agreement of any kind. Not all that glitters is gold; the grass is not greener on the other side, and there is more to a book than its cover. Look deeper, beyond vanity and face value to the heart of all things. Then, and only then, will you truly see what it means to be beautiful.

REVERSED

Reversed, the *Seven of Cups* suggests you are being frivolous with your resources or are gullible and easily persuaded because you are too reliant on external gratification to satisfy an emotional void you feel within. A heart in a constant state of wanting will starve under the weight of gluttony. When you find contentment and happiness from within, you will notice how you no longer crave 'stuff'. You will become fed up with the sheer quantity of objects in your possession and commit to a mass purging. A phase of minimalism is being called for. By learning to live with the resources you have, you will find—paradoxically—that you become more resourceful and have more energy to give to yourself and others.

This card's shadow signifies promiscuity and unhealthy sexual attachments, causing drama and complications. It leaves you feeling weak as you give away your power, turning it into an unsacred exchange. Alternatively, this energy manifests as selfishness, where you simply neglect to offer emotional support out of indifference, making you a bad friend and unreliable support system. Reflect on your recent actions — have you been selfish? Open your life to fresh air and vitality. Reach out to a friend, engage in rewarding charity, practise active listening and eye contact, and ground and centre your energy daily to become more present and aware.

Narrative

The Charlatan is always at the market without fail, peddling his wares. A cunning salesman, he is a predator behind a table of jewels. To fall into his trap is to lose your hard-earned money. He will make you desire things you never considered before and feel you can't live without his trinkets. Once he convinces you to buy one item, he'll persuade you to buy another until you leave his tent overloaded with purchases. Many people have fallen victim to the Charlatan, yet it's rarely his fault. It's very easy for somebody to tell you what you need, but it's up to you to determine what brings value to your life and discern want from need. It's easy to blame the Charlatan, call him names, and question his accountability. But at the end of the day, the Charlatan teaches us an important lesson — we are each free to choose. Our ability to do so is a powerful gift.

Correspondences

» **Astrology:** Venus in Scorpio

» **Major Arcana:** *VII The Chariot, XVII The Star*

Journal Prompts

» Are you materialistic? What does materialism mean to you?

» What do you know about the minimalism movement? Would you consider it?

» Do you prefer new items or antiques? Describe your relationship with new and old.

» What emotional connection, if any, do you feel towards your personal possessions?

Morgana
EIGHT OF CUPS

MORGANA

Eight of Cups

Embark on the odyssey of letting go, a pilgrimage for truth. Find fortitude in spiritual journeying.

IN A READING

The time has come to begin an odyssey. You may feel spiritually dissatisfied as if there is more out there. Begin a pilgrimage to truly nourish that part of yourself that seeks deeper meaning. This is the call of the seeker. Such a feeling is sacred and should be honoured to the best of your capacity. Abandon outdated projects, however fruitful they have been. It's time to deepen your understanding of the bigger picture. Searching for emotional equilibrium through spiritual means will prove beneficial for you.

It might involve making conscious, ethical changes, such as the call to a cruelty-free diet. Or, you could volunteer your time and energy for a cause you believe in. This moment is a natural ending of old, shallow ways of living and a time to move on. This brush with divine timing is an act of serendipity.

Reversed

You have an inability or lack of desire to leave a situation when all arrows point to the exit. Sure, there are times we are just not ready to let go, suggesting there may be stubbornness here. But you feel now is simply not the right time to embark on an odyssey. The desire may be there, but the timing is not right. Such a realisation is quite frustrating as if life is passing you by. Maybe you're realising you are returning to what was once left behind. Check in with yourself — have you returned to your old ways out of a longing for emotional pleasures? If that's what you need, fine. But be mindful, as you may be in danger of repeating old patterns. However it unfolds, trusting in the Universe will ease your concerns about moving on from what doesn't serve you anymore. You'll be okay, you'll be safe, and things will improve — just take a deep breath and let go of trying to control everything. Remember, the world is full of possibilities beyond your bubble. Stay open to new experiences and start by taking small steps to explore the world beyond your comfort zone.

Narrative

Morgana is beginning her pilgrimage to the Sacred Isles. There, she will begin her training as a priestess of the old ways. Such a journey is not as easy as it appears. There are many miles between her home and her destination, and a great deal of doubt may easily creep in as she begins her travels. She wonders how her mother and sisters will fare without her. Will she be forgotten? Will she be remembered kindly? What if she forgets her family and upbringing? Her young heart is a storm inside her chest. She aches for clarity and support. But, alas, she is heading into an unknown place devoid of certainty, and she can take no one with her. When she emerges again, she will be a priestess of the old ways, revered everywhere. All will know her name.

Correspondences

- » **Astrology:** Saturn in Pisces
- » **Major Arcana:** *VIII Strength, XVIII The Moon*

Journal Prompts

- » What does a 'spiritual odyssey' signify to you?
- » In what ways do you find yourself seeking deeper

insight into the world around you, and how does this desire shape your daily experiences?

» What aspects of travelling bring you the most joy?

» In what ways have you experienced relationships where connection was missing?

PEACOCK QUEEN & THE ELIXIR OF LIFE

Nine of Cups

Embrace the gift of happiness and spiritual love, pursuing change for the better. Beware overindulgence, find satisfaction, and celebrate abundance with gratitude.

IN A READING

Something you have been wishing for will soon come to pass. There is great happiness in this card — emotional satisfaction, genuine fulfilment, and an honest belief in the power of love. It heralds a time of blossoming, where the heart is fuller than ever and bursting with goodness. Engage in random acts of kindness, and dance, sing, and express your joy in ways others can observe and revel in.

The *Nine of Cups* signifies the love of luxury. It serves you to have a healthy vanity and enjoy the finer things in life. Comfort is a focus for you now, particularly if you have struggled in the past. Your reliance on material possessions for a sense of happiness is real but only temporary. Understand that true happiness is not a result of any possession but the mark of a peaceful spirit. Lasting relationships are what prove to be incredibly fulfilling. If thoughts of marriage and civil union are dancing around your head, enjoy the idea of cementing a bond with the person you love. Embrace practices that enrich your state of being, and honour them with focus and consistency. Doing so means you are living consciously, with purpose and meaning.

Reversed

Unsettling relationships tax you. When experiencing difficulties and challenges with a loved one or a close friend, be sure to respect yourself enough to walk away when the time comes. It may not fix the underlying issue, but it will give you—and others—the space to find the energy and resources to help you work through it. These kinds of situations are indicative of a generalised state of lack. You may desire more comfort and more resources, yet you cannot act on any plan that may bring you closer to your desired result. Outline your goals in detail on a sheet of paper. Then, one at a time, take each goal and break it down into practical steps. Ask a friend or two to help you gain perspective and refine your objectives. By the time you finish this task, you will have an outline of a path aligning your ambitions and goals in a practical and achievable way.

Another way this sense of lack may show up in your life is through wastefulness. When you feel emotionally unfulfilled, it's common to try to fill that void with material possessions, thinking it will satisfy the deeper needs you're ignoring. However, acquiring more 'stuff' won't truly satisfy what's missing. By addressing the core feelings of dissatisfaction or emptiness, you can break this cycle. Practices like mindfulness can help you reconnect with what you truly need rather than turning to fleeting material distractions. In doing so, you cultivate a more balanced and genuinely fulfilling life rather than constantly chasing what's next.

Narrative

After a hundred-year drought, the villagers rejoiced as it finally ended. They had prayed fervently to the higher power they believed in. But the village elders instead took offerings to the river to petition the Peacock Queen.

They knew it would take more than a mighty rain to break the drought, so they set to work to create a banquet for her. Once all was complete, they placed a basket fit for the goddess on the river and waited and sang for nine days and nights. On the tenth morning, she appeared brilliant in her plumes and resplendent in her nature, carrying the Chalice of Life, sacred and powerful beyond measure. As the Peacock Queen poured its contents onto the villagers, the parched lands around them sprung to life, revealing a lush cornucopia of beauty. From that day on, the rains were commonplace, as were the offerings to the Peacock Queen.

Correspondences

- » **Astrology:** Jupiter in Pisces
- » **Major Arcana:** *IX The Hermit, XIX The Sun*

Journal Prompts

- » In what ways do you find yourself making wishes?
- » Describe a time when you felt a wish had been fulfilled.
- » If you were to crystallise your favourite emotion, how would you describe it, and why is it meaningful to you?
- » How do you perceive the idea of a higher purpose?

THE LUNAR CUP

Ten of Cups

Embrace your happiness with both hands and claim it wholeheartedly. You are entering a time of genuine fulfilment and deep emotional connection.

In a Reading

You have reached the pinnacle of joy after great sorrow, and a phase of lasting happiness is about to begin. The heart is lighter, the smile cannot be wiped from your face, and you are bursting with joy. It could be a time of harmony within your family, where quarrels that may have existed are now definitively over. It could also present as a time of great success — your hard work has paid off, and you may have attained your goals. You should feel very proud of yourself. Reaching a goal is indeed a special moment and a mark of your perseverance, character, and strength of will. A new phase begins, and within it is born the opportunity to re-establish the kindest versions of yourself.

The catalyst for such a state may be nothing more than peace, serenity, and perfect simplicity. Through mindfulness and refining your processes, you begin to understand the importance of simplicity. Too much, and you don't know what to do with it; too little, and you feel as though you are going without. The euphoria of such a pure moment will no doubt leave a lasting impression on you. Look at your capacity for love, sorrow, and forgiveness, and learn about yourself and your emotions. Such knowing is indeed wisdom. Happiness lies in the balance of all things, and the *Ten of Cups* is a sign that lets you know you have achieved that balance in your life. So please, celebrate.

Reversed

Even in a reversed position, the *Ten of Cups* is still an extremely positive card of happiness and wholeness. It suggests you cannot see the blessings staring you in the face. Open your eyes and your heart to the wonder of the world around you. Work on cultivating a deep gratitude practice. Gratitude is profoundly healing and possesses the transformative ability to reshape your outlook. By reframing your thoughts to acknowledge the blessings already present and those yet to unfold, gratitude becomes a catalyst for profound shifts in perspective.

Narrative

The wild and ancient moon is a clever shapeshifter. At times of great power, when the moon is full and blood red, the Lady herself steps forth, changing her shape to herald a sign. It is said the Goddess herself drinks out of the sacred chalice, her lips touching its form. The mere sight of it is breathtaking. Those who walk the path of the old ways recognise such a sign in the sky. There is a quiet understanding. Those who know have many reasons to rejoice, for the Lunar Cup is no small sign. The Lunar Cup, or Great Chalice of the Lady, marks the beginning of peace in a world of chaos. It is the time to drink, love, and laugh in her name, rejoicing in the splendour of a cycle of harmony.

Correspondences

- » **Astrology:** Mars in Pisces
- » **Major Arcana:** *X The Wheel of Fortune, XX Judgement*

Journal Prompts

- » What does happiness mean to you?
- » What would it take for you to be truly happy right now?
- » What is one of your greatest aspirations?
- » If you could bless your entire family with a gift, what would that gift be?

Kuan Yin
PAGE OF CUPS

KUAN YIN

Page of Cups

Embrace your gentle side as a strength while honouring your intuitive faculties, and remember to be compassionate.

IN A READING

The *Page of Cups* invites you to connect with your inner world, fostering emotional and intuitive growth. It marks a period of openness to self-discovery through creativity, deepening relationships, or spiritual expansion. This card encourages transformation through curiosity, sensitivity, and receptivity.

To navigate this time, engage deeply with your inner world. Start with mindful practices like journalling or noting moments that spark curiosity. Explore creative or reflective outlets such as painting, meditation, or quiet walks in nature. Embrace vulnerability in relationships and practise honest communication. If heightened sensitivity overwhelms you, use grounding techniques like barefoot walks, deep breathing, or spending time outdoors. Set healthy emotional boundaries to protect your energy and find balance. By nurturing your growth, you invite clarity, stronger connections, and greater self-awareness into your life. Embracing this journey opens the door to a more authentic, compassionate self and a life full of understanding, connection, and possibility.

As a Person

The Page for the water element is a dreamy character with the sweetest of smiles who loves easily and completely, revelling in the emotional high of interconnectedness. Tender of heart and mind, she makes a great listener, offering kindness and understanding even in the face of challenges. Fond of causes centred on compassion and healing, she embodies softness and gentleness yet shows enthusiasm for imaginative and artistic pursuits. Her romantic nature often leads her to view the world through rose-coloured glasses. At times, she may seem off with the fairies, employing selective hearing, which can be a bit frustrating for the speaker. Nonetheless, her big heart and compassionate demeanour more than make up for these shortcomings.

Reversed

When reversed, the *Page of Cups* suggests you are entering a phase of emotional vulnerability, where sensitivity and sentimentality may dominate your experience. Feelings of discomfort or sorrow may arise, often triggered by unresolved insecurities or emotional imbalance. Whether this is from envy, spiritual confusion, or romantic obsession, the root cause usually lies in disconnection from your inner emotional stability.

To navigate this phase, take time to sit with your feelings and reflect on why certain situations trigger you. Ask yourself what lies beneath these reactions and explore any unresolved emotions. If jealousy arises, question why you feel threatened by the success of others — turn this energy into self-reflection, not comparison. If caught in fantasy or drama, ground yourself in reality by seeking balance. Reconnect with your own values, taking small steps to regain clarity. Practise self-awareness in your interactions, especially with loved ones, ensuring your conversations and focus remain authentic. By fostering emotional regulation and introspection, you'll unlock a sense of inner peace and stability, enabling you to move forward with purpose.

Narrative

Since childhood, Kuan Yin, the Daughter of Compassion, saw the world through the lens of empathy. Her extraordinary ability to feel the suffering of others led her to face life's storms so that others wouldn't have to endure them. Her fearless compassion caught the gods' attention, who summoned her to meet them.

Though honoured, her parents feared for her wellbeing. They accompanied her to plead with the gods for protection, but the gods initially refused. Instead, they offered her the chance to stay in the realm of gods and spirits. Kuan Yin declined, unwilling to abandon a world in pain or her grieving parents. After deliberation, the gods agreed, but on the condition that Kuan Yin would join them only once the world was free of sorrow.

To this day, Kuan Yin lives in the hearts of those who embody kindness, peace, intuition, creativity, and compassion, forever offering solace to those in need.

Correspondences

» **Astrology:** Cancer

» **Elemental Combinations:** Earth of Water

Journal Prompts

- » Describe how you are compassionate or where you feel deeply sensitive in your life.
- » What does intuition mean to you?
- » Explain your thoughts on the subject of gossip.

LADY OF THE LAKE

Knight of Cups

From passion to vulnerability, from allure to insecurity ... embrace each feeling as a step towards a deeper connection.

IN A READING

You are going through a phase of deep feeling and profound nuances, provoking the romantic in you and finding yourself in a state of unfolding — specifically, an unfolding of the heart. You are ready to engage in a romantic relationship. This same energy also manifests as the burning desire to immerse yourself in the world of art, culture, and music. Engaging in storytelling and active listening is a beautiful pastime that honours the sacred in all things. Tune into the sacred and walk an intuitive path. Feel inspired to make conscious decisions and strive towards a meaningful existence. This intense heart energy wants more from interactions and experiences than what is presented at face value. It compels you to do the right thing. Think and act with compassion and sympathy, and your heart will be nourished by all it desires and grow to share its power with all around you.

As a Person

As a person, this perpetually romantic Knight is charming and idealistic — in love with love and fascinated by moving and inspiring artistic works. She avoids conflict at all costs, preferring instead to listen and be kind, considering the situations of all parties in order to mediate effectively. Such a compassionate character proves to be a wonderful healer in situations of emotional conflict. When passive mediation fails, she claims power and sovereignty by using cunning emotional tactics.

Some might call this archetype seductive, others might comment on her pleasing aesthetic. Regardless, she exudes something quite mysterious and enigmatic. Her outer landscape does not mirror her inner one. There is a world of magic, power, and mystery behind her eyes. Soft-spoken and with subtle grace, her gentle demeanour should never be confused with weakness. She is valiant, chivalrous, and will go to arms in the defence of a cause. When her will is applied, she has great influence and can manoeuvre a situation into a favourable position without resorting to manipulative methods. She is the knight in shining armour.

Reversed

Reversed, the *Knight of Cups* can be impractical and temperamental. As such, you may find yourself in a state of avoidance, refusing to confront situations that need your attention. You don't yet understand the feeling of disconnect present within you. And yet, the impulse to act on this largely misunderstood feeling is a powerful presence. This can lead to escapism — be mindful of your crutches and the fundamental lack of discipline. You cannot commit to projects or provide support if your behaviour is flaky, unreliable, and untrustworthy. If you resort to manipulative tactics to gain the upper hand during an emotionally challenging time, just stop. You know this feels wrong to you, but the reaction you are getting is everything you want and so much more. Such behaviour runs thin in time and will cease to be effective and become exposed. Honesty is always the best policy. Healthy communication is encouraged. When you embrace healthy communication, kindness and understanding naturally follow. Engaging in open and honest discourse can profoundly benefit your healing journey.

Narrative

They say the Lady of the Lake dwells beneath the water, but such is the way with gods — their tales are rarely as they seem. What you must know is that she's an ancient deity born before time itself. She's the keeper of countless stories, having witnessed the rise and fall of kings, empires, and the magic that shaped them. Monarchs and magicians have sought her mirrored counsel, sharing their secrets and seeking her favour.

For a long while, she held the balance of power, subtly shaping the destinies of kingdoms. Though rarely seen in battle, she championed her causes with ruthless efficiency. Some misunderstood her — but remember: she hails from a primal time when knights duelled, magic thrived, and the world danced to a different rhythm. She holds the secrets of magic, the thread that binds all worlds. Even today, those who gaze into the waters may sense her presence, encountering something older than time itself.

Correspondences

- » **Astrology:** Scorpio, Mercury
- » **Elemental Combinations:** Air of Water

Journal Prompts

- » What do you do to bring harmony to your space?
- » Would you describe yourself as a compassionate individual? If so, describe your language of compassion.
- » Describe your emotional insecurities.
- » Where in your life do your creativity and imagination thrive?

YEMANJA

Queen of Cups

Explore the depths of sensitivity and intuition, from empathy to enchantment, from introspection to warmth. Embrace the journey, weaving through the realms of emotion and spirituality, nurturing connections along the way.

IN A READING

Demonstrative of enduring compassion and deep sentimental feelings, you are in a deeply emotional and spiritually awakened phase, sparking your imagination and expanding your unfurling heart. This is transformative, and the answer is simply to surrender. Kindness and empathy are the gifts you have that you can share with others. Such heart-expanding openness attracts emotionally fulfilling romantic relationships into your life.

This open heart attracts you to beauty, so you may find yourself pulled towards objects and artworks that you recognise hold an inherent beauty that is impossible to describe with mere words. Be present in the transcendence of material objects into timeless, universal wonders, and you will be inspired to create and share all that is beautiful. Music, visual art, culture, nature, and many other subjects are fountains of inspiration, enticing the muse to come through you.

This is also why many who are touched by the *Queen of Cups* find themselves on the path of the priestess. When your heart is open, intuitive and psychic experiences trigger an awareness of the numinous. Such a path leads to a mysterious road that winds like the river to the sea. This inner calling leads to heightened senses and a feeling of coming home.

As a Person

As a person, the Queen of the watery realms represents a sensitive individual, demonstrably kind and compassionate. Others will gravitate to her for the kindness and compassion she gives so freely. She is the archetypal mother — constantly caring for others and ensuring those in need are always well-supported. For this reason, this person may be the type of individual to gravitate towards social services and compassionate causes. Here, she is of value to others who require support to grow and heal. You will most likely find her in a healing role, perhaps as an art therapist. She is naturally intuitive and may appear otherworldly or mysterious. Your eye will be drawn to her for her grace and beauty. She is the type of individual who loses herself in interests relating to spirituality and art because her driving force is soul fulfilment instead of material gain.

Reversed

The reversed *Queen of Cups* signifies a time when your heightened sensitivity may cause you to react impulsively to emotional triggers. You may feel disconnected from your sense of purpose, lost in moodiness and disorganisation, and struggling to find balance. This imbalance prevents you from connecting with your higher self and the sacred path. Shift your focus from external expectations or material gains and instead seek satisfaction within — true success lies in aligning your goals with your inner desires, not in pleasing others.

To navigate this phase, embrace action over daydreaming. Instead of getting lost in idealised notions, take concrete steps towards your goals. Acknowledge that the reality of your situation may not match your fantasies, but moving forward is key. Combat procrastination by grounding your energy and focusing on one objective at a time. With determination and mindfulness, you will regain clarity and achieve the fulfilment you seek. Embrace this period of introspection and be proactive in bringing your dreams into tangible reality.

Narrative

Some say Yemanja was born of the ocean; others say she is the ocean. Some say she is the keeper of the womb of life; others say she is the blood that courses through every vein, both physical and metaphysical. They look to her as mother, but more than that, they yearn for her comfort, understanding, and compassion. She is grace, wisdom, and divine creation. All she touches is sacred. She is said to claim your dark and unwanted pieces, washing the shards of your splintered soul clean before returning each sacred and purified piece to your heart and soul so that you are once again magnificently whole. The waters of the ocean are a piece of her. For eons, men and women lay offerings for her at the water's edge, adorning rocks and sand in her name, all to receive her blessing. It was believed her blessing would protect you your whole life. Should any malevolent energy seek to cause you harm, they would suffer her wrath to the bitter end.

To bathe in the waters of her creation is to purify completely, aligning the body to enter a state of divine flow. Priestesses of the ancient world were drawn to her. When the moon was full, they would journey to the water's edge, revelling in the sound of the ocean ... waves crashing ... wind raised. There, alive and powerful by the water, in rituals as old as time itself, these ancient priestesses would petition Yemanja for her divine aid. And there, at the water's edge, they would receive her blessing in the form of enhanced wisdom, psychic ability, divine imagination, perpetual nourishment, compassion, and deep enduring love. Such were her blessings for all humanity.

Correspondences

- » **Astrology:** Cancer
- » **Elemental Combination:** Water of Water

Journal Prompts

- » Describe a moment that felt genuinely psychic to you.
- » How often do you rely on your intuition?
- » Describe your regular spiritual practice.
- » Describe the areas of your life where you tend to procrastinate.

POSEIDON

King of Cups

Embrace emotional balance and compassion, stepping into deep empathy and insight. Navigate the human heart with wisdom and grace.

IN A READING

The *King of Cups* represents a time of emotional inspiration and connection, encouraging you to share your creative energy and empathic nature. This card calls you to help others grow while nurturing your own relationships through loyalty, respect, and care.

To make the most of this energy, offer your expertise to support someone else's personal growth, whether through guidance or collaboration. Focus on fostering harmony in your relationships by avoiding conflict and embracing maturity. Show your affection and appreciation through thoughtful actions, deepening emotional connections with those you care about. Allow yourself to be loyal and vulnerable, recognising the strength in these bonds. By focusing on collaboration and nurturing relationships, you will create an environment of trust and emotional fulfilment. Your efforts will build stronger connections, bringing lasting joy and deep satisfaction. Embrace the opportunity to grow together with others.

As a Person

This King represents a highly motivated, calm, and friendly individual with the best intentions. He makes you feel genuinely heard and encourages your endeavours because he truly believes in you. He offers wise counsel, avoids conflict, and is respected by all. His charming demeanour creates a sense of comfort and peace, and he easily reaches the middle ground to ensure cooperation. People are drawn to his energetic charisma and optimism, seeing good in all situations. He prefers deep, meaningful conversations over idle chitchat. He is a brilliant father figure you seek for direction, assisting you in finding the confidence to achieve your goals through your own intuition, making him a wonderful guide and teacher.

Reversed

This is a critical phase where you cannot muster a compliment. Instead, you find yourself with an inner restlessness that makes you more judgemental. Are you perhaps being too controlling with a tendency to be overbearing? Be sure to moderate your issues of control by being mindful of your triggers. Understand that individuals need space to breathe to express themselves effectively. Becoming overly emotional only alienates you from those people who matter most.

Also, be mindful of constantly comparing yourself to others. Looking to another and their accomplishments proves detrimental to your peace of mind. We are all on a journey, and it is not a competition. Take the time to understand your unique value in this world. What special skills do you possess? What do you have a particular aptitude for? Focus on your strengths and channel them into your goals. Keep your eyes on the prize, and don't let yourself be distracted.

Narrative

Poseidon has a foul temper. He controls earthquakes, tempests, and terrible sea storms that lead to perilous conditions. Magnificent in his appearance, he is larger than life and commanding. His legend was created aeons ago and has been twisted over time to represent the motives of those seeking to utilise his legacy as an aid or a weapon. But every story has its truth, and the story of Poseidon is no different.

He fell from the holy place into the waters below. So at home was he that he chose to make the seas his kingdom. It is said that water lacked life prior to being claimed by the god. Now, water is a living ecosystem and a cunning beast in its own right — one moment, it is completely tranquil and terrifying in its power in the next. There is no telling what water will do, so it is unpredictable, mysterious, relentless, and deserving of much respect. Such is the nature of the god of water.

The inky-blue depths of all bodies of water are Poseidon's domain. To anger water is to anger the king. A great many ships have lost their way due to misdealings and cruelty in his kingdom. It is nothing for the king to reach up and simply take down a ship. He smiles upon those who honour the water, assuring smooth passage across any river, lake, or ocean. He can ensure an abundant catch and clear sky, but more than anything, he ensures the safe return of any traveller by water.

Correspondences

- » **Astrology:** Pisces, Neptune
- » **Elemental Combination:** Fire of Water

Journal Prompts

» Describe a challenging moment during which you exercised control over your emotions.

» How understanding are you?

» Do you consider yourself a good shoulder to cry on, and why?

» How are you at giving compassionate advice?

Minor Arcana

Kingdom of Wands

Soul fire is the spark of life and magic that ignites the World Tree and ensures its life for all time. It is the creative force that transforms into brilliant colour and incredible sound. To hear the whispers of the World Tree is to breathe in a creative force and a sacred magic that gifts you with success in all that you do. It sets your soul on fire and transmutes you into a divine creator.

In the Bonestone, soul fire is represented by the suit of Wands.

Element:
Fire

Polarity:
Masculine

Astrological Signs:
Aries, Leo, Sagittarius

Season:
Summer

Cardinal Direction:
South

Minerals of Resonance:
Fire agate, jasper, pyrite, Larimar stone, Herkimer diamond, obsidian, Apache tears, kunzite, kyanite, jade, iron, ivory

Botanicals of Resonance:
Asafoetida, angelica, bay, cinnamon, cinquefoil, dragon's blood, carrot, chilli, juniper, mandrake, garlic, galangal, clove, rue, saffron, St John's wort, wormwood, tobacco, pepper, pennyroyal, nutmeg

THE SERPENT FIRE

Ace of Wands

From the spark of ignition arise new beginnings. Transcend creative limitations and embrace initiative with enthusiasm.

IN A READING

Magic is at work in your life, so be open to the creative force — access to spiritual power is in your hands. Harness its potent ability effectively and put into action what is needed. Your ability to create on a sacred scale is now at your disposal, and you need only take the first step towards actualising your dreams. It all begins with that first step. To do this, honour the divine flow. Take hold of the creative moment where ideas flow through you at a rapid rate. Grounding even one of these ideas makes a powerful start towards successful outcomes in your endeavours. Be aware though — you may feel overwhelmed. That's why it is necessary to plan and create a solid framework for any endeavour that you are about to pursue. Whether this is a new venture or a budding enterprise, your quest to create something tangible lies in your ability to manage that creation effectively.

Reversed

You experience a creative block due to distraction and stress. As such, you are unable to see the creative force at work in your life. This stops you from pouncing on the opportunities that lead to successful outcomes. This reversed card also indicates potential setbacks and failures in achieving your goals. Such setbacks eventuate in a lack of focus and confidence that is detrimental as you work towards achieving your dreams. Relieve your tension and cultivate focus so you can recover quickly from any setbacks hindering you thus far. Creative fatigue is real, especially when attempting to apply ideas that were once successful but have now run their course. An injection of positive, vibrant, and creative energy is necessary to mitigate the problem at hand.

Narrative

This serpent is sacred. It represents life force and the divine creation of the universe, all rolled into one scaly, sentient being. It is as old as the dragons who breathed volcanic molten fire during the creation of the universe.

The serpent is a symbol of the wild and unbridled side of nature. Creation and destruction all rolled into one.

The sacred serpent is considered the totem of the Magician. Fire is not constant — it must be invoked in one form or another. To dream of the serpent means your path is beginning to unravel. You will need to play the part of the grand creator. To see the symbol of the serpent in the form of the ouroboros—the snake eating its tail—is to know that your path to completion lies in your first steps of creation.

Correspondences

- » **Astrology:** Ascendant and/or Point of Aries
- » **Major Arcana:** *I The Magician, XI Justice*

Journal Prompts

- » What happens when you cannot act on one of your creative ideas?
- » When have you experienced a creative block?
- » When do you receive your best creative ideas?
- » Do you feel you have a creative spirit?

FLAME BUD

Two of Wands

In co-creation and individuation, dynamic energy propels pioneers forward as cooperation becomes the driving force behind initiatives for advancement.

IN A READING

The *Two of Wands* signifies taking initiative to shape your destiny. It calls you to reclaim your power and embark on a grand, creative adventure driven by that dynamic force fuelling your desire to create. Celebrate your individuality with intense, innovative action. Assess your skillset, acknowledge your strengths and weaknesses, and consider seeking another to help fill the gaps. Cooperation proves beneficial in the success of your endeavours. This card is also a welcome sign to reclaim your sovereignty, so individuation plays a rather large part in this process. At some point, you have to make some critical decisions on this path. You are the hero of your story and are more than capable of gaining dominance over a situation. Find the confidence to ensure this transition benefits you by embracing your unique vision and stepping boldly towards your goals. The confidence you build during this process will enable you to navigate challenges with clarity, make decisive moves, and foster collaborations that amplify your creative power. Ultimately, this will lead to personal growth, and the satisfaction of seeing your ideas come to life. Rise to the occasion and reclaim your power by aligning your will with a higher purpose.

Reversed

The *Two of Wands* reversed finds you at the mercy of another or feeling flooded with feelings of helplessness. Remember, you are in connection with divine power at every moment in your life. Find your voice and speak your truth. Articulate your boundaries and non-negotiables clearly and concisely. Doing so inadvertently educates others on how you wish to be treated and garners their respect.

It also indicates the inability to cooperate with others, leading to detrimental situations where arguing, confusion, and ill wishes become the status quo. Don't get drawn into situations that are inherently divisive or even violent. Alternatively, it may be your ego that has surpassed acceptable levels, asserting your dominance in inappropriate ways. Examine your behaviour and motivations closely to determine whether you are still the right person for the job. Be honest with yourself and respectful to others moving forward — it demonstrates good character.

Narrative

The woodland creature Flame Bud has been possessed by the creative force, the spark of life. He knows well what he must do, so he sets out in search of his purpose. With staff in hand and an astute pixie guide, he sets off to explore the vast expanse of land that awaits. While he lacks the map, the destination, and the information necessary to grant him a sense of peace during his travel, he knows he will get there by the will of the gods. You see, my friends, Flame Bud is an optimist. He does not question the whys or hows. He simply allows the creative force to guide him forth. With courage in his heart, he takes step after step. Alongside his pixie companion, he embraces the open road and the world of opportunity that awaits.

Correspondences

» **Astrology:** Mars in Aries
» **Major Arcana:** *II The High Priestess, XII The Hanged Man*

Journal Prompts

» What does 'power over' mean to you?
» Describe what cooperation feels like to you.
» How do you find working alone compares to working in a group?
» How are you at asserting your will?

CILLA
Three of Wands

Patience births progress, wisdom refines ambition, and from the ashes of disappointment, the phoenix of realisation shall rise.

IN A READING

The *Three of Wands* is a card of great vision, of determination. It carries an intense energy of radiant vitality that can be applied to any project, thus ensuring its success. For example, you may be inspired to create a business plan or a strategy that can be applied to your project. Such achievements lead to tangible rewards that continue to inspire you onwards. In the face of this, calm and patience are required. Sometimes, we work towards projects diligently and do all that we can. Other times, the only thing left is to wait patiently and hope our efforts were enough. And so, hope is yet another aspect of this card. Hope elevates our perspective, pulling our thoughts from the pessimistic valleys of our minds, so a brighter outlook is achieved simply by shifting perspective and elevating our vibration. Combining virtues leads us to successfully completing a project and expanding our endeavours, which in turn becomes a powerful catalyst for immense achievement. In this state, our thoughts become magnetised and capable of attracting beautiful experiences into our lives.

Reversed

There is restlessness or hopelessness towards an endeavour. Stop second-guessing yourself and believing you could have done more or better. This type of twisted hindsight is of no benefit to you. When you find yourself embroiled in worry—perhaps even fear—for an outcome or situation, remember you have more control than you believe. Living in the past doesn't help either. If you are constantly triggered by regret and a wish to go back in time and do things differently, stop pondering on past events and start looking towards how wonderful things will be when you are living your best future. When your worry is tied to the outcome of the project, it serves no purpose and must be cast aside as a non-productive emotion, a hindrance to the vitality of the endeavour. Step into a space of assuredness, embracing the power of confidence that comes with the shift. Stand firm in your power and remain in a constructive headspace — here is where success takes shape.

Narrative

Cilla gazes intently through her telescope, her eyes fixed on the canvas of the future unfurling before her. The very essence of adventure courses through her being as she embraces a secret rite of passage reserved for the valiant and audacious. From this vantage point, a fresh perspective of the world reveals itself, bathing all in a new light. Slowly, like a map unfurling within her mind's eye, her path takes form, each step illuminated by the wisdom that arises from deep within her very bones. This truth, forged in the crucible of her experiences, solidifies into a guiding beacon, becoming a catalyst propelling her towards the horizon where her destiny boldly awaits. Amidst the expanse of clouds and the enchanting blue sky, she floats, a harbinger of direction and purpose. Joined by kindred spirits bound by a shared vision but destined for diverse destinations, Cilla becomes a manifestation of courage and determination, a testament to the power of embracing the unknown with unwavering resolve.

Correspondences

- » **Astrology:** Sun in Aries
- » **Major Arcana:** *III The Empress*, *XIII Death*

Journal Prompts

- » Describe a recent success.
- » Describe a time when the excitement of beginnings was felt in your life.
- » Describe a current creative endeavour.

THE BLESSING

Four of Wands

In life's grand melody, harmony conducts the celebration of completion, yielding the sweet fruit of prosperity.

IN A READING

The *Four of Wands* is a sign of great celebration, a point of tremendous achievement you can openly acknowledge. You have endured challenging circumstances in order to attain your success, which should be treated as an incredible accomplishment. This is indeed a joyous occasion and should be celebrated in kind, so revel in the fruits of your labours and acknowledge it with a deep and satisfying out-breath. Thus, it also symbolises the marking of time and the recognition of significant dates such as weddings, birthdays, and anniversaries. It is a nod to the harmony in the hearth, a time of genuine bliss felt in your household. Rest after everything you've experienced, and you will enter a time of peaceful sleep, full bellies, and hearts full of love.

Reversed

The *Four of Wands* in reverse suggests a lack of structural solidity and gain. For example, this framework might be intangible, like the beginning phase of a project, relationship, or business partnership. You may feel disheartened and restless, ready to abandon a project you've worked on diligently without progress or reward. Carefully examine the structures around you or your endeavours to ensure their stability helps engender success. If you believe in something's potential, adjust your methods, expectations, and approach to reinvigorate it with fresh energy. If not, surrendering it can create space for something more aligned with your authentic self. Additionally, reflect on whether you feel adequately honoured and valued in your life. A lack of recognition disrupts stability and diminishes your spirit. Seek or create rituals that celebrate your milestones and reaffirm your worth, either through personal practices or by fostering community connections that uplift and support you. You need to feel sacred and valued as much as anyone else. It is the community's job to come together to honour the spirit of each soul in the group. When you align your actions with your true purpose, stability becomes established, and the fires of your creativity are rekindled. This is your opportunity to build a stronger, more fulfilling path ahead.

Narrative

In a rite as old as time, the matriarch of the bloodline weaves botanicals into the crown of the maiden. This is a moment of blessing, of celebration and its acknowledgement through refined acts of love and honour. The matriarch knows this blessing all too well, for she, too, had received such a blessing in her maiden years. It was the most joyous occasion, where tribes from all over came together to celebrate and rejoice. Great alliances were made that proved the foundation of fortune and the cementing of a legacy of sovereignty for the tribe. The matriarch gently and thoughtfully braids each botanical into her granddaughter's hair. She fastens it with a prosperous blessing so that her granddaughter may excel in life and claim her sovereignty when the time calls for it.

Correspondences

- **Astrology:** Venus in Aries
- **Major Arcana:** *IV The Emperor, XIV Temperance*

Journal Prompts

- When was the last time you gathered people around you for a celebration?
- How is building a solid foundation important to you?
- In what ways have you experienced or missed out on important rites of passage in your life?

THE REDWOOD CHALLENGE

Five of Wands

In the arena of life's drama, competition fuels the fires of ambition and creative conflict. Embrace struggle as an opportunity, turning chaos into focused energy.

IN A READING

Prepare for some friendly competition. It is a rare moment in our lives when we are able to succeed and rise to accolades without a bit of friendly competition. Competition helps refine our skills and uncovers a powerful thirst necessary for igniting our inherent ambitious qualities. This can, however, lead to conflict with another in a situation where there is a little push and pull to determine who has the upper hand. Assert your will and focus your energy in a clear direction with enthusiasm, igniting the fire in your belly. At times, it is channelled emotions that give life to projects. Injecting constructive and passionate energy into something propels it along, leading to success. The *Five of Wands* also signifies a strange sense of optimism. While there may be difficulties and conflict, a little gumption and a whole lot of optimism will take you far. These attributes assist you in standing out in a crowd, gaining the upper hand.

Reversed

A competition that started out friendly has now gotten a little nasty. This may result from ego or hidden motives — either way, there is no longer a level playing field. With this card reversed, you are at the mercy of unscrupulous tactics and quiet manipulation. You may be the victim of backstabbing and/or naysaying, or your rival seeks to gain the upper hand through duplicitous means. Be mindful of what you say now and to whom you say it. It seems not everyone has your best interest in mind. Stand firm and enforce your boundaries. It may be wise for you to gather evidence that can be used later strategically. We can't always win them all, but we certainly can lose with dignity. Our attitudes during times of defeat highlight the type of individual you are. Be mindful of being a sore loser.

Narrative

Ará and Quell, born of fire's essence, step forth as luminaries seeking more than just mastery with the bow. Their journey takes them across the ancient primordial landscapes of Bonestone & Earthflesh, a path carved by determination and an unquenchable desire to be tested. Fire thrives in the heart of competition, and they find their true calling in the face of challenges. Their pursuit is not merely a display of skill — it's a testament to the enduring human spirit, a reminder that the pursuit of excellence is a lifelong journey. With every drawn bowstring, they ignite a spark of inspiration, reminding us that within the trials of competition lies the forge of human potential.

Correspondences

» **Astrology:** Saturn in Leo

» **Major Arcana:** *V The Hierophant, XV The Devil*

Journal Prompts

» In what ways do you experience competition in your life?

» How do you navigate competitive environments?

» How do you respond to chaotic situations?

» What are your greatest strengths?

THE SOVEREIGN SELF

Six of Wands

Leadership emerges amidst the pursuit of happiness and strength, transcending the illusion of control.

IN A READING

The *Six of Wands* is a sign of victory — recognition for your efforts and celebration of your and others' deeds. It is a truly powerful moment when you recognise your sovereignty and decide to honour it. Enjoy your achievements, immerse yourself in well-deserved pleasures, and bask in the spotlight of recognition.

New opportunities reveal themselves to you. Lean into your self-confidence, allow it to guide your decision-making, and you will know what to do when the moment arises. You are exactly the person for the job. There is no second-guessing here; there is no shyness or lack of self-worth. There is only confidence, desire, and the will to achieve that which you set your mind to. If you have any doubts, it is time to identify your fears and work towards overcoming them so that you may reach that long-awaited victory. An outside perspective will help you see your situation from a different angle, so confer with trusted allies, and new solutions will emerge. Now is the time to be courageous and step forth with purpose. No one can hold you down, and no one will keep you from your destiny.

Reversed

You are dissatisfied with your lot in life and have squandered an opportunity that you now regret. You feel jealous, bitter, or resentful of those now living their true purpose. But, one missed opportunity does not define you. When you make a pact with yourself to embrace your next opportunity, it will come your way. Set an intention to focus on yourself for a period of six months. Make a concerted effort to achieve as much as possible to propel yourself forward. Make yourself a priority and focus on your wellbeing. Let practicality meet soul-nourishing spirituality and take charge of your direction now. Embracing practices and routines that help you achieve brings much-needed enjoyment and peace into your life.

Narrative

There comes a time when everyone must rise to the occasion. This is a moment of honest self-evaluation where ego has no place in the decision. Merit and accomplishment are the only guiding forces here and, of course, the will of the Divine. Before there were kings, chiefs, or leaders of any kind, there were the gods, and it was they who deemed the first man or woman to be crowned. So, by their own hand, a crown was fashioned of many earthly treasures, and a declaration was spoken out loud. This declaration affirmed their sovereign right. And so were born the first kings and queens, the first leaders of the ancient tribes. Crowned by their own hand but made solid through their merits.

Correspondences

» **Astrology:** Jupiter in Leo

» **Major Arcana:** *VI The Lovers, XVI The Tower*

Journal Prompts

» Describe a time in your life when you truly felt victorious.

» In what area of your life do you exhibit the most pride?

» Describe a goal you are striving towards.

» How can you avoid regret by seizing the opportunities that are handed to you?

THE BLADE WITCH

Seven of Wands

Stand firm against overwhelming threats with tenacity and valour and embrace the mantle of advocate and warrior in the face of challenges.

IN A READING

Take a firm stand on a matter that you wholly believe in. When you truly care about the outcome of a situation, you must be prepared to advocate for it with your heart and soul. The *Seven of Wands* is a clarion call to find a cause to champion or spearhead a campaign of the heart. This aligns you with a strong sense of purpose, which is pure nourishment for your soul. You are drawn to assist in problem management because you can handle small crises and are incredibly talented at simultaneously managing multiple situations. You are exactly the person for the job, so have no fear of any sense of inadequacy. It might require a rapid and intuitive response, so you will have to deal with any situation in the moment. While you may feel unprepared, trusting your good judgement will take you far. Repeat to yourself: "Embrace the unknown, trust my instincts, and adapt with confidence." This mantra reminds you of your capability to handle whatever comes your way and empowers you to excel in any circumstance.

Reversed

Encountering the reversed *Seven of Wands* signals a caution against stubbornness and single-mindedness. It's a reminder to pause and honestly evaluate your motives. Are you pursuing your goals out of a genuine desire for the greater good, or are selfish desires clouding your judgement? Take the time to seek input from trusted individuals who can provide valuable perspectives outside your own. True strength isn't just about persistence — it's about being flexible and self-aware enough to adapt when necessary. So, stay open to alternative paths and be willing to reassess your approach. Through this humility and openness, you'll find the true pathway to success and fulfilment.

While you may feel unqualified for the task at hand, you are not. This sense of inadequacy breeds hesitation and undermines your self-confidence — but your heart knows the truth, and with it, a shame that triggers aggression. It may be buried under layers of fearful experience, but your courage is within you — you need only find the pathway to it. To find it, start by acknowledging your fears and doubts. They are natural, but they don't define your capabilities. Reflect on past experiences where you have overcome challenges or stepped out of your comfort zone. These moments serve as evidence of your resilience and courage.

Narrative

The Blade Witch is always prepared for a fight. She never backs down and is the fire that urges her army ever forward into the fray. Her heart is pride itself; her blood is valour. Every action and every deed is well thought out and executed for one purpose: war. The men and women in her legion are always astounded by her tenacity on the battlefield. She knows no mercy. Her eyes are always on the prize. And she never returns home with anything less than a shining victory. She is legendary.

Correspondences

- **Astrology:** Mars in Leo
- **Major Arcana:** *VII The Chariot, XVII The Star*

Journal Prompts

- Describe a cause that is near and dear to your heart.
- How do you fight for what you believe in?
- Describe a time when you demonstrated tremendous courage.
- Describe a time when you struggled to find courage.

WILD HORSE

Eight of Wands

Wild Horse
EIGHT OF WANDS

Embrace the divine creative spark within you and summon your will to take inspired action. Movement and change are needed right now, so be ready to make your move.

IN A READING

This is a time of bold action, fuelled by a passionate heart that knows exactly what it wants. When the *Eight of Wands* appears, there is love to be found. The type of love that is tremendously transformative, the type of love that moves mountains and makes the impossible possible. This love needn't be romantic, but it is bold and all-consuming, like a lightning bolt electrifying everything it touches. It is a divine spark that drives you. Muster up every ounce of energy and focus on your desired outcome. To do this effectively, have a very clear image of what you want to achieve. You must be ruthless in your pursuit of it. For this, you will require both strength and stamina. The payoff for your single-minded pursuit will exceed your expectations of success. And, better yet, you may end up surprising yourself.

Reversed

This card reversed suggests your efforts lack stamina, and you feel lethargic in pursuing your goals. Perhaps you are wasting too much time on hesitation and second-guessing, or your lack of stamina is simply due to laziness. Either way, it's your attitude that is the hindrance here. Define your goals, write them down on paper and determine the steps needed to accomplish each task. Turn each step into action and see how things rapidly change around you. You will be achieving this in no time. You need only begin.

On the other hand, don't overdo it. Overwhelmed by a project's pace, you might rush and make critical errors, or it may be your nature to hurry through tasks without attention to detail. Be mindful of this and slow things down a little, look over the finer aspects, and relish the feeling of a job done well. You may be given ample time to accomplish your goals; however, you are wasting that precious time by procrastinating. Create a schedule for yourself and organise your work area into a distraction-free space. Set achievable deadlines and hold yourself accountable for meeting them. Look at something like the

Pomodoro Technique, for example, which helps improve focus by using timed work sessions with breaks. A solid grasp of time management lessens your stress significantly and allows you to be in control of your responsibilities, leaving you feeling extraordinarily powerful.

Narrative

Wild Horse is regal. It is indeed a tremendous honour to be able to ride one. It is said that the spirit of the Wild Horse is one of true divine consciousness. To climb up on their back is to be taken on a great odyssey at a speed through which all of life blurs. The rapid nature of this journey is said to wash the rider clean of all that holds them back. After such an odyssey, one emerges with clarity of mind, focus, and a passionate heart. This is how people are made. The Wild Horse is a powerhouse of strength. Every stride is measured. Their stamina is incredible, and they do not easily yield. It is said that when a Wild Horse bows their head at you, you are their kindred spirit. They will bond with you and your spirit for the remainder of your life.

Correspondences

- » **Astrology:** Mercury in Sagittarius
- » **Major Arcana:** *VIII Strength, XVIII The Moon*

Journal Prompts

- » Describe yourself in love.
- » Are you a person of action? Describe your approach to problems.
- » In what ways do new projects spark excitement for you?
- » Describe your attention to detail.
- » How do you stave off procrastination?

The Green Woman
NINE OF WANDS

THE GREEN WOMAN

Nine of Wands

When you stand dedicated, your resilience and resolve intertwine, helping you stay the course in the pursuit of enlightenment.

IN A READING

The *Nine of Wands* is a card of great inner strength, of a strong spirit, and of profound sincerity. This is the card of the divinely guided. Take a defensive stance in a tense situation. You may be urged to focus carefully, ensuring you do not unnecessarily waste your energy because the unfolding situation may take time.

Adaptability is yet another key aspect of this card. You are urged to think on your feet and modify your approach constantly. This may be a challenge to begin with, but you will find a sense of ease, and over time it will become second nature. There is as much patience in this card as there is action — a measured approach. Endurance and strength of character are required when we choose to dedicate ourselves to a cause. By being adaptable, you'll find it easier to handle life's changes and challenges. Over time, this flexibility will help you grow and find a balance between taking action and being patient.

Reversed

Someone close to you might be showing resistance, which is disheartening. Rather than feeling stuck, consider adjusting your approach. Explore new ways to navigate the situation and be patient with yourself during this trial-and-error phase. Persistent solutions will emerge, allowing you to overcome the frustration.

You may also encounter contradictions in your interactions. In these moments, clear and caring communication is essential. By expressing yourself calmly and thoughtfully, you avoid misunderstandings and help others understand you better. If you expect the worst, this might stem from underlying fears or anxieties. Remember, not every challenge is destined to fail. Practise mindfulness, challenge negative thoughts, and embrace gratitude. This will help you shift towards a more positive outlook. Spending time in nature may help you feel grounded, bringing peace back into your life. Through patience, clear communication, and a positive mindset, you will navigate these challenges and emerge stronger, more centred, and ready to face whatever comes next.

Narrative

The Green Woman was the keeper of the sacred forest. For eons, she stood in defence of this sacred place and every sentient being therein. Never had she faltered, never had she left her post, and never had she been derelict in her duties. Year after year, century after century, eon after eon, she stood. Until, at long last, the forest finally claimed her as its own. Now, she is indistinguishable and completely camouflaged by her kingdom. And there, she lies in wait.

Correspondences

» **Astrology:** Moon in Sagittarius

» **Major Arcana:** *IX The Hermit, XIX The Sun*

Journal Prompts

» Describe an old wound that may be hindering your progress in some way.

» In what ways do you show your flexibility or inflexibility in life?

- » Describe your approach towards goals. How dedicated to them are you?
- » When have you had cause to take a defensive stance?

DIGGER

Ten of Wands

Digger
TEN OF WANDS

You are burdened with great responsibility. Now is the time to muster your strength and persevere despite exhaustion. Determination is a necessity.

IN A READING

This card suggests a drastic change. Identify what no longer works for you. Your time of struggle is nearing an end. Overcome by obligation and burden, you feel exhausted, but the appearance of the *Ten of Wands* marks a cycle drawing to completion. While the cycle is ending, you still need stamina to persevere, considering the sacrifices made thus far. This final effort may feel the most laborious, but ending the cycle and liberating yourself is necessary. Focus on self-care and indulge in simple pleasures to relieve stress. These struggles may be self-inflicted, pushing past comfort or feeling overwhelmed by deadlines and expectations. Instead of dwelling on the cause, take brave and inspired action: renegotiate deadlines, cancel obligations, and prioritise self-care. Practise sacred selfishness, set boundaries, and rebuild your strength. With time and effort, the best of you will emerge to face a bright new day. Summon the strength and stamina to restructure your life and make changes that actually improve things for you. The changes you want to see can only happen if you take action to make them happen.

Reversed

You are completely overwhelmed by responsibility and are running on empty. You may have invested time, energy, and precious resources into a single goal while neglecting your other obligations. This causes strain in different areas of your life, such as more friction than usual in your relationships. With nothing more to give, you have run out of strength, and your health may be waning. You may be taking more than you are giving, and your attitude and approach may be wearing thin. Attempting to fulfil your obligations at this moment in time is diminishing your quality of life. Stop being the martyr and exaggerating your suffering or constantly complaining to others about your burdens. Being challenged every step of the way, you feel quite emotional. Take a step back to reassess your priorities. A simple shift in perspective holds the potential to relieve the pressure.

Narrative

He was known as Digger on the battlefield. Trustworthy and dependable, he would never dream of leaving behind a fallen brother. Those around him depended on him. His kind heart and his honour placed a tremendous burden upon his shoulders. Not only was Digger there to fight, but he was also there to retrieve any fallen warriors. He was the only one bound to such a duty. It was a tremendous responsibility to carry, a responsibility that became a burden. Nevertheless, he did not complain, nor did he question his lot in life. He simply put one foot in front of the other and hoped for the best while enduring some of the worst. When asked where his motivation came from, he simply responded, "The war will not continue forever. One day, it will be over and I can return to my fields again."

Correspondences

» **Astrology:** Saturn in Sagittarius
» **Major Arcana:** *X The Wheel of Fortune, XX Judgement*

Journal Prompts

» Describe a time when you felt burdened by circumstances out of your control.

» What would it look like if you could make a drastic life change?

» Do you have a tendency to take too much on? Describe your current workload.

» Do you tend to finish that which you set out to achieve?

IANSÁ

Page of Wands

Iansá
PAGE OF WANDS

In the dance of life, swift enthusiasm meets assertive inspiration, shaping you into a purposeful leader — where artistic willpower is guided by tempered wisdom.

IN A READING

The *Page of Wands* heralds an exciting project, perhaps the opportunity you have been waiting for—to express yourself creatively for a project meaningful to you—or perhaps you have neglected your creative side. You are being called to a far more creative path, and the time has come to nurture your divine creativity. The enthusiastic energy of this card helps you harness your full potential, so get ambitious! You may need to get a little bit aggressive, a little bit hungry, to achieve the things you desire. This does not mean you need to play dirty — it simply means you must be creative, cunning, and charming to get what you want. This card signifies a radiant sensuality that sparks your creativity. This passion could lead to encountering your muse, a romantic relationship, or a new lover. The spark of your adventurous spirit leads you in search of a meaningful adventure. When the mood strikes, embrace it fully. Welcome the fiery breath of ecstatic change. The door to adventure, both within and around you, opens wide, heralding a new chapter in your story.

As a Person

The fiery Page represents an excitable character who brings a passionately creative approach to any situation. She is charming, expressive, and speaks with her entire body. Warm-hearted and kind, she can also be quick to anger, leading to rash consequences. Despite her pride preventing an apology, she seeks to make amends through heartfelt and creative means. Known for her charm, she excels in relationships, creating intense connections but often burning through lovers quickly. However, she will fiercely honour her true love. Ambitious and sometimes cunning, she prefers to work smart, dedicating herself to meaningful work. When lacking purpose, she may appear flaky, but this indicates a need to seek better opportunities.

Reversed

When the *Page of Wands* is reversed, it may appear as if you are fickle and insensitive. The truth is that you are ungrounded and detached. This restlessness has you acting unpredictably, being impulsive, always desiring more success or gratification, or being erratic and volatile in a relationship. Now is a time for grounding and connection.

Establish a mindfulness practice that helps you stay present and appreciate the wisdom of the moment. Pause, observe your feelings, and address their root cause rather than reacting to symptoms. Reassess what you genuinely desire. Focus on balance and ground yourself in what truly matters to avoid being consumed by unhealthy pursuits. Chances are your fire is burning people, so take the time to get honest feedback about how your actions affect others. Then, find a professional to help you tether yourself back to a shared reality. Set yourself firm boundaries and communicate openly. By reconnecting with yourself and facing your emotions honestly, you can find the stability and depth you seek, setting the stage for meaningful growth.

Narrative

Iansá is a force to be reckoned with. She is divine and formidable. Born of a fierce tempest, her heart beats to the rhythm of the war drum. Her desire for action is often mistaken for recklessness. She does not care for the opinions of others, nor does she allow others to get in her way. She is self-led, some might say divinely led. No matter how you look at it, there is something incredibly unique about this woman — powerful, eager, fierce in her approach. Her spirit is indomitable, and her heart is bold. She will fight for her causes and inspire others to do the same. She leads if she must, but only if she must, preferring instead to work independently as she sees fit. She may be rash, but her heart is immense. Her desire to do good is never-ending. But her temper … well, it has been the gruesome undoing of many a foolish foe.

Correspondences

» **Astrology:** Aries, Leo, Sagittarius
» **Elemental Combinations:** Earth of Fire

Journal Prompts

» What situations in your life are you truly excited about?
» When was the last time you felt a passionate fire burning within you?
» How much emphasis do you place on your creativity?
» Describe a time when your ambition may have gotten out of hand.

HEPHAESTUS

Knight of Wands

With forthright power and sultry allure, ignite the path as a skilled leader, navigating the wild with honourable devotion, shunning recklessness for cunning resolve.

IN A READING

The *Knight of Wands* signifies a vigorous call to action.

Now is the time for a drastic life change. Now is the time to embrace something that truly gives your life meaning. Anything else will simply not do. Embrace your passions in ways that require a fearless attitude and strive for your dreams. Seize the desire to do something unconventional yet incredibly fulfilling. Push aside the status quo in favour of adventure. Nurture your uniqueness and allow it to inspire you in ways you may have never dreamed of. This is the time for you to question what you truly want. You need to be prepared to throw yourself in 100 percent as you strive for your goals. Unleash yourself into the world — it needs someone like you. No one else can do what you can do. When you give yourself full permission to be the incredible human being you are and offer your skills out to this world, the world around you will change.

As a Person

The Knight of the fire element is a revolutionary character, undoubtedly like no one you have ever met. He has a natural and passionate intensity that is a little too much for the average person. Nevertheless, he is a charmer—and a good-looking one at that—with a steady confidence that makes him irresistible. He may be as sporty as he is creative, with energy to boot. He is both a lover and a fighter and is not fond of commitment. This does not mean he will never commit; it simply means he will change his ways the moment he meets 'the one'. He often appears as a knight in shining armour and has a way of always being the hero.

Reversed

The *Knight of Wands* reversed suggests you've been waiting for the perfect moment to start something, but endless contemplation has delayed your progress. Waiting for everything to align perfectly only keeps you from living your dreams today. It's time for bold action and change.

It's time to move forward with purpose, even if it feels like a leap of faith.

Define your goal clearly and take one tangible step towards it, no matter how small. Acknowledge your fears, but don't let them twist you up. Fear leads to anxiety and a restless spirit, so counteract it by engaging in activities that bring you joy and fulfilment. Build a routine that grounds you, and resist the urge to compare yourself to others — your journey is just as unique. Trust that each action you take will bring clarity and momentum, even if the path isn't immediately clear. By stepping out of your comfort zone, you'll discover resilience and a renewed sense of purpose. Now is the time to invest in yourself and move forward with confidence — you are capable of achieving more than you imagine.

Narrative

Hephaestus was a fabled blacksmith living in a cave, far removed from the wealth and decadence of the civilised world. Many travelled great distances to seek his skill, for in those days, a blacksmith was seen as more than a mere craftsman — he was a magician. Metal was believed to possess its own spirit, a living god in its own right, and only the hands of a master could shape it into something worthy of kings. Hephaestus' creations were legendary;

no sword he forged ever shattered, no shield ever cracked, and no armour was ever pierced. His craft was divine, yet he was as discerning as he was skilled. Hephaestus refused to work for just anyone. Those who wished him to fashion metal for them had to bring more than gold; they had to bring a story worth telling.

Kings, queens, and nobles made countless offers, desperate to claim him for their courts, but Hephaestus valued his freedom above all. He had no desire to be tethered to a throne. His art was sacred, something he would practise only when and how he chose. For him, freedom meant the ability to follow his own path, to create only for those who truly inspired him. Then, one seemingly ordinary day, a stranger entered his cave with a request unlike any he had heard before. As always, Hephaestus asked for the man's story. When the stranger inquired why it mattered, Hephaestus explained that a person's story was their legacy, which must be folded into the metal to give it life. The stranger smiled, not fully understanding, but he appreciated the sentiment. When he cast aside his cloak, a brilliant green light filled the cave, and Hephaestus realised this was no ordinary man — it was a god. And on that day, in the quiet of his cave, Hephaestus set to work crafting wings for a forgotten god of the old world.

Correspondences

- **Astrology:** Sagittarius, Mercury
- **Elemental Combinations:** Air of Fire

Journal Prompts

- Describe a unique facet of your personality.
- In what areas of your life do you demonstrate passion?
- Describe a time when you allowed fear to hold you back.
- Describe a time when you had to power through fear in order to succeed.

MARIE LEVEAU

Queen of Wands

Marie Leveau
QUEEN OF WANDS

Stand firm in your power, embracing the allure of your creativity. Be kind and compassionate yet steadfast in your resolve.

IN A READING

You are entering a phase of confident achievement, being given the opportunity to exert your creative force to achieve something powerful. Exuding a certain level of sensuality and charm may be necessary to gain another's favour, or you might need to dig deep into your fiery arsenal to connect with the fiery queen within you. You may also feel the need for genuine self-expression through creative means. However it presents for you, the *Queen of Wands* is a catalyst for greatness, urging you to connect with the vibrant energy of life that courses within you. It stimulates the visionary in you as you enter a creative time, where what you are channelling is needed and, therefore, must be shared. Adjust your life to ensure your lifeforce flows fully and completely through you, both physically and metaphysically. Consider adopting a short meditative practice that focuses on peace and gratitude. Take the time to nourish your body and incorporate meaningful movement to encourage soulful flow. Have you ever tried fire dancing? You may even find yourself drawn to methods of expression that are uncharacteristic of you yet precisely what you need. Embrace the spirit of creative adventure and allow yourself to go with the flow, choosing the path of inspired action. Doing so will help to fill your proverbial cup.

As a Person

The Witch Queen is beguiling, effortlessly moving through life with the grace and poise of a true queen. She appeals to many, and her appearance delights the senses. The way she speaks, the tone of voice, the way she moves … all demonstrative of a powerful arsenal capable of bringing a kingdom to its knees. She is an incredibly capable visionary. Her ability to turn a dream into reality is one of her greatest skills. She is fantastic at fundraising and generating interest in any project she sets her mind to. Whatever she touches turns to gold. She loves a good party and enjoys fine food, music, and drink. A conversation with her tends to be profoundly riveting, as she immerses herself in meaningful exchanges that ignite a passion in others. In fact, most walk away from such a conversation with a new understanding of what truly fuels them.

She has a natural way of inspiring greatness in others; thus she makes a brilliant coach. Warm, friendly, and longingly affectionate, when she loves you, you know it. She is a natural champion of causes and will not hesitate to advocate for another. When crossed, she makes a formidable opponent.

Reversed

The *Queen of Wands* reversed suggests a compulsive attitude. Your compulsion may be born out of impatience and an inability to know your limits, or you struggle with the concept of control — attempting to control another, or perhaps it is the other who is controlling you. This attempt to control may be difficult to detect. It could be through seduction, emotional hooks, or sexual pleasure. Nevertheless, the end result is to gain power over another. Cultivating authentic connections is essential. Prioritise compassion and understanding over manipulation. Reflect on intentions and practise openness and empathy in interactions. By prioritising collaboration and mutual respect, we foster spaces where love and kindness flourish, creating deeper connections with those around us.

Narrative

They came to see her, the Witch Queen Marie Leveau, in droves. She had cultivated a reputation over an unnatural span of time. No one knew her age nor where she came from. The only thing they knew about her was that she was a woman of magic. When she walked down the street, the world was divided. One half was in awe, the other in fear. With a polarising force around her, those who loved her loved her well, and those who feared her came to love her eventually. Naturally captivating, her eyes held the secrets to the world. Poised in her knowing, she smiled at a world taken with her beauty.

Those who sought out her particular skillset were as charmed by her demeanour as they were by her work. She worked calmly and confidently, with unparalleled skill. She never faltered or failed. For this reason, her reputation grew and spread throughout the community like wildfire. Soon, everyone wanted to come and meet *the* Marie Leveau.

Feared and adored, her admirers numbered in the hundreds and comprised the most affluent individuals. It was difficult to resist her charm because when you looked into her eyes, she discerned things you didn't know and yet wanted to know desperately. Sooner or later, everyone in the region had walked through her abode. Sooner or later, she learned everyone's dirty little secrets.

Correspondences

- » **Astrology:** Leo, Venus
- » **Elemental Combinations:** Water of Fire

Journal Prompts

- » Describe a time when you felt jealousy towards another.
- » How do you connect with the *Queen of Wands*?
- » What does the term 'visionary' mean to you?
- » Describe an instance in your life where you have felt a magnetic attraction.

SUN GOD RA

King of Wands

When your willpower and dynamism meet, the fire of purpose ignites, driving you to take assertive action towards spectacular horizons.

IN A READING

The *King of Wands* gives you a divine push, inspiring you towards your goals. Embrace the challenge of self-actualisation and assertive effort. Taking on aspects of leadership, harness your integrity, optimism, and enthusiasm. You will need to innovate and assert your authority in a manner that leads to confidence and fairness. Action speaks louder than words, and so it will prove the most effective way of solidifying victory. Engage in activities that harness your creative potential. Using pen and paper, do a brain-dump activity, noting the various creative ideas swimming around your magnificent mind. From this, fully formed ideas will emerge. These will prove to be beneficial to others on a grand scale, making you a pioneer. This comes naturally to you because you have the necessary skills to handle this situation without compromising your integrity or morals. Simply be yourself and show people what you can give. Your generous attitude and calm confidence attract those needing direction because you are a beacon for those seeking advice and your expertise. Ready yourself with a variety of ideas, suggestions, and advice. The direction of prosperity will change in your favour when you fully enter your leadership role.

As a Person

This King represents an igniting individual with a natural charisma that lights up a room. He is warm and friendly and oftentimes the natural centre of any party, which is why others are drawn to him. Whether by choice or encouragement, he seems to always land himself in leadership positions — some might say, the only position that truly suits him. He does not squander his authority or use it in egotistical ways. People tend to get excited about his new ideas, which are often a money-spinner, as he has a way with words that makes others feel impassioned and excited to be part of any project he puts together. He usually has a regal demeanour, holding space for many simultaneously and never failing to make others feel heard. He is also a bold adventurer with the heart of an explorer and a leader who doesn't hesitate to act when called to do so. This is a passionate combination and a catalyst for an emerging true hero. Fierce in the pursuit of greatness, but never at the cost of another, he has an unwavering love and enduring loyalty towards his loved ones.

Reversed

It's time to take a cold, hard look at your attitude towards others. This might be a difficult phase, but asserting your authority and being aggressive and domineering is detrimental to your relationships. It might be time to get back to your roots and remember what once inspired you. When situations don't go your way, that flare of anger has brutal consequences, which is why you need to find ways of releasing your anger without jeopardising the peace of others. Focusing on your health and fitness would help — run, swim, walk, dance, or practise a primal scream in a safe space. There are many constructive ways in which you can self-soothe. Find one that works best for you and, in doing so, invite more peace into your life.

Narrative

Oh, how he blazed: Ra — King of the Sun. Born of its fiery ripple, he poured out onto the sand and took form soon after, beautiful, alluring, and captivating. He walked with conviction, intense in his way, his eyes smouldering with a hint of fire flickering within. Some say he was born fully grown; others say he was raised from a babe to a man. But no one truly knows the stories of the gods, so they say a great many things.

Nevertheless, what is known of him is impossible to ignore. He holds sway over the very sun in the sky and moves to a solar rhythm. You would think a being with such magnificent capabilities would be a tyrant, but not so. The Sun God Ra was every bit as human as any other. Never seeing himself as more, he didn't seek to gain dominance. He was perfectly content in his position, knowing all the while that if there was anything he wanted, anything he needed, he only had to ask, and it would be given to him. But did he ask? No — instead, he chose to give warmth, light, and life to those in need. His energy was enchanting, and it was easy to become entranced when you saw him. He flowed with a natural sort of light and a gentle smile that was dazzling even to the blind. He was felt as much as he was seen. A born king, it was his destiny whether he wanted it or not. And while this truth was undeniable, he was in absolutely no rush to build a throne and be crowned king. He believed in his heart that every person was their own ruler, and humanity was not there to be ruled. He determined that people needed to be inspired and guided, activated to be ushered into their greatness. With this realisation, he began his work — he decided to be the Sun to all.

Correspondences

» **Astrology:** Aries

» **Elemental Combinations:** Fire of Fire

Journal Prompts

» What is your relationship with fire?

» How do you associate with the *King of Wands*?

» Describe your favourite pioneer.

» Write down your three most important goals, then ask the *King of Wands* how to achieve them.

Minor Arcana

Kingdom of Pentacles

The root, the trunk, the branch, the leaf — manifestations of life and sacred solidity. Bone, stone, earth, and flesh are manifestations of the earthly kingdom and the divine form they have been given. Bonestone & Earthflesh make up the sacred building blocks of life. They form the immense and unfathomable structure of the Great Tree.

In Bonestone, sacred solidity is represented by the suit of Pentacles.

Element:
Earth

Polarity:
Feminine

Astrology Signs:
Taurus, Virgo, Capricorn

Season:
Winter

Cardinal Direction:
North

Minerals of Resonance:
Bone, petrified wood, amber, smoky quartz, tourmaline, moss chrysanthemum stone, emerald, jet

Botanicals of Resonance:
Beet, cotton, cypress, fern, patchouli, mugwort, vervain, rhubarb, wheat, honeysuckle, tulip, corn, buckwheat

MANDRAKE SPIRIT & THE SKULL OF THE OLD ONE

Ace of Pentacles

Prosperity flourishes when you honour the solidity of earthly beginnings, treasure the gift of physical health, and nurture the sanctuary of home.

IN A READING

The *Ace of Pentacles* signifies fortune and a new beginning. This is a positive step towards solid material gain. This could even prove to be the beginning of your accumulation of wealth. It's also a fantastic omen for those engaging in business, suggesting it will flourish and a true abundance of resources will be available to you. To welcome the prosperity of this card into your life, take practical action aligning directly with your goals.

Send the résumé, speak with a financial adviser, or begin a feasibility study for your business idea. Whatever the action, beginning is the primary objective here. All of this brings a sense of security, whether it relates to a financial situation or a romantic relationship. Draw attention to your health and nurture your physical body to ensure you work towards optimum health. Think holistically, and create an opportunity to nurture your mind, body, and spirit. Self-care is a pact you make to ensure you invest time, energy, and resources in your wellbeing. Self-care requires commitment and discipline — you need only apply yourself.

Reversed

The *Ace of Pentacles* reversed warns of the coming conclusion to a positive streak of financial gain. You need to conserve your resources. Carefully construct a workable and honest budget to ensure you understand where you are financially so you don't deplete your resources. Understanding your actual financial position grants you a certain measure of security. Materialism is a rather prominent theme in your life, as you place more value on possessions than your health and relationships. Embrace a phase of minimalism and prioritise experiences over material possessions. When you simplify your life and resources, you will feel lighter and find it easier to manage.

Narrative

The Skull of the Old One has never decayed, turned into powder, or faded away. Instead, something else took place — the spirit of an ancient green-world ally grew through the skull, one that would become the totem spirit of witches. The skull guarded the Mandrake Spirit. It set in place an impenetrable barrier of energy that the naked eye could not see yet could be felt by the physical body. The power of this shield soon began to attract a great deal of attention. Many came in search of it. They used it to measure strength, might, manhood, and sovereignty.

But Mandrake Spirit cared not for such things. It was in search of a pure heart. On the eve of the new moon in Taurus, a little girl stumbled through the forest and happened upon the Skull of the Old One and the Mandrake Spirit. Curious, she caressed the plant, which responded and quavered under her touch. Enchanted, she attempted to pull it out from the root, a mighty feat for such a little hand. And yet, she managed. As soon as she did, another mandrake root popped out of the earth — exactly in the place of the mandrake she had removed. When the girl returned to her village with the root in her hand and presented it, her mother smiled and said, "Now you are a witch, and the green world is yours to safeguard. Beware the will of humanity, for not all possess a noble heart."

Correspondences

» **Astrology:** *Medium Coeli* or the Midheaven (MC)
» **Major Arcana:** *I The Magician, XI Justice*

Journal Prompts

» Describe the most beautiful thing you have ever seen.
» Describe how you demonstrate financial responsibility.
» What is your relationship with your material possessions?

THE RAINBOW SPIDER

Two of Pentacles

Make balancing agreements a part of your day. The spirit of balance depends on multitasking, productivity, and flow.

IN A READING

It is time to learn how to balance responsibilities, prioritise tasks, and carefully multitask to maintain the order and flow of a situation. In order to expand on your resources, apply yourself in ways you may not have needed to before. Consider planning and organising your time more effectively or create a budget to determine what resources you have at your disposal. Make no mistake: time is a valuable resource, just as valuable as money. When you do the work, you can level up relatively quickly. Productivity is key, and productivity is heavily reliant on good time management. Extend this balance to your body, and ensure you cultivate healthy habits. Learn to move gracefully, feel harmony, and understand your strengths and limitations. Investing time and energy into matters of the home and family benefits everyone, and connecting with the natural flow of things, both within and without, leads to better outcomes.

Reversed

The *Two of Pentacles* reversed signifies a phase of lethargy. Your productivity may be at an all-time low, or you may have overextended your resources and are now concerned about not having enough. Or, you may be neglecting your home, family, loved ones, or managing your resources. It's no wonder you feel a little discombobulated like you have lost your rhythm. These are all clear signs that things in your life are probably out of balance. Finding flow can be challenging when society is constantly in flux and rapid motion. We don't all have a peaceful home and space in which to relax and just *be*. Many of our lives are fast-paced, and it's easy to drop the ball from time to time and feel out of touch with our unique rhythms. Grounding and centring exercises will help you reconnect. Walk barefoot upon the earth, consume root vegetables, or work with the magic of stones, such as smoky quartz, ruby, or (my favourite) tourmaline. The goal is to regain focus to restore a sense of order. You will notice how juggling competing demands becomes effortless again when you feel grounded and present to yourself.

Narrative

The Rainbow Spider was born with a unique symbol on its back; a symbol said to belong to the realm of the ancients. The Rainbow Spider became a symbol of great power. It stood for sacred balance and the ability to complete tasks at an astounding rate. It is said that if you find a Rainbow Spider in your home, a particular series of events will unfold. Your environment will become extremely busy. Opportunities will begin flowing in and out. You will be required to attend to every detail simultaneously, and you will not be able to rest until every task is complete. Should you manage to fulfil your obligations and complete each task in a timely fashion, the blessings of the Rainbow Spider will be yours. Your home will forever be a place of harmony and flow.

Correspondences

- » **Astrology:** Jupiter in Capricorn
- » **Major Arcana:** *II The High Priestess, XII The Hanged Man*

Journal Prompts

- » Do you find multitasking to be effective?
- » Describe your approach to organisation.
- » Look at your life at present and determine where it is out of balance.
- » Describe your natural rhythm.

Sacred Stone
THREE OF PENTACLES

SACRED STONE

Three of Pentacles

The meaningful fusion of talents creates a strong foundation for teamwork. By harnessing your teams' skills, your creativity, productivity, and achievement are assured.

IN A READING

There is a joyful, creative aspect to the *Three of Pentacles* — pleasure in the work being done. In fact, your task looks less like work and more like the joyful pursuit of a creative endeavour that is destined to be fruitful. Perhaps it is the early stages of a project taking form, something you have been working towards. But this form is rough and rudimentary and requires further shaping. Perhaps now is the time to collaborate with other skilled creators to help bring your vision to fruition. Teamwork is a powerful solution. Through healthy teamwork, you can open to new perspectives that enhance your original vision. You can also lighten the workload and move through your tasks with speed and ease.

Reversed

This card reversed signifies the necessary reorganisation of plans and projects, meaning you have to sit down and take a cold, hard look at your resources and ensure you have a solid planning structure in place. If you are going through an unproductive phase, this could be due to a lack of enthusiasm or boredom in an endeavour. Remind yourself that there are many stages to completing a goal, and not all of them are necessarily glamorous. Attending to the boring details is the equivalent of ensuring that the creative engine runs smoothly. It also allows you to revise your work — take the time to dot the i's and cross the t's. There is magic and strength in a well-oiled machine. Be sure to do your due diligence to avoid unwanted surprises. Get down into the nitty gritty and familiarise yourself with all the moving parts to develop better-functioning systems to improve productivity and compliance.

Another meaning highlights your apprehension or feeling unworthy of your position due to not accepting your full worth. Your current position has come to you through hard work, so you deserve it. Remember, every success, every accomplishment, and every opportunity you've earned reflects your capabilities, dedication, and talents. Embrace your achievements with confidence and acknowledge your worthiness. Surround yourself with supportive individuals who recognise your strengths and accomplishments, and remember to celebrate your victories, no matter how small they may seem. And most importantly, be kind to yourself.

Narrative

The carving of the sacred stone is not a small task. Those responsible for etching the divine symbols were chosen at birth and taught the ways from a young age. It is said that you could have every skill necessary to complete this sacred duty, and yet you may still fail. You may fail because the stone has its own life force, its own mind, and a story that defines it. So, part of the skill of carving the sacred stone is knowing how to listen to the ancient whispers of the stones themselves — only then should one attempt a carving. By mastering this skill, one creates a work of art that stands the test of time and is revered for centuries.

Correspondences

» **Astrology:** Mars in Capricorn
» **Major Arcana:** *III The Empress*, *XIII Death*

Journal Prompts

» What projects are you currently working towards completing?
» How well do you work in a team environment?
» Describe your productivity flow.
» In what ways do you nurture your natural talents?

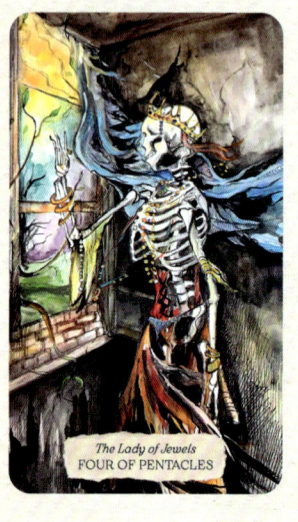

The Lady of Jewels
FOUR OF PENTACLES

THE LADY OF JEWELS

Four of Pentacles

Reject the desire to covet material resources to feel more secure. Prosperity and abundance require the open flow of giving and receiving.

IN A READING

The *Four of Pentacles* signifies the danger of holding on too tight after achieving stability. Despite all your resources, you are still in a state of dissatisfaction with your lot in life. You have achieved something beautiful, financially and materially. However, it is not the time to rest on your laurels. Perhaps you have been investing too much time and energy in accruing wealth and resources and not living life to the fullest. Pause briefly and gather your strength before proceeding to your next goal. Define your goals right down to their core. Understanding your motivations gives you insight into your core self, which proves profoundly healing. Progress requires stepping out of your comfort zone and adapting to changing circumstances. Trust in your ability to navigate challenges with resilience and determination, keeping your sights on your long-term objectives. Because of this card's link to material wealth, it can also suggest new resources coming into play. There is no need to be frugal here. Instead, decide to utilise your resources wisely so that they can multiply.

Reversed

The reversed *Four of Pentacles* signals a release from the rigid need for control, whether over your finances, possessions, or health. Where the upright card represents clinging to resources, in reverse, it invites you to loosen your grip and reassess what truly matters to you in the here and now. This can manifest as letting go of materialism, being more generous, or adopting a more flexible mindset around wealth, health, and stability.

However, it also warns against going too far — reckless spending or lacking attention to important responsibilities can lead to further instability. It's crucial to strike a balance between holding on too tightly and carelessly letting go. This card asks you to take responsibility for your financial health and wellbeing, ensuring you're not avoiding important matters. As you release control, you create space for new opportunities, growth, and a more authentic sense of security.

Narrative

The Lady of Jewels was once a creature of fame and fortune. She had materialised her every wish — and every wish was boldly materialistic. She wished for a beautiful home, for dazzling jewels, and for mountains of wealth. She received all of her wishes and, in doing so, became so obsessed that she refused to leave her dwelling. She never went outside to engage with life, preferring instead to remain in her home, admiring her belongings and enveloped by her treasures. Her presence in the community dwindled. For a while, people wondered where she was, but no one bothered to seek her out. Years passed, and no one remembered her, her peculiarity, or wealth of belongings — no one remembered her at all. And while the world continued to turn, the Lady of Jewels faded into oblivion. She remained in her house, an empty shell, just bones. Bones adorned in jewels. For the love of all her things, she gave up her life.

Correspondences

- » **Astrology:** Sun in Capricorn
- » **Major Arcana:** *IV The Emperor, XIV Temperance*

Journal Prompts

- » Describe an area of your life where you play the part of a miser.
- » How competent are you at managing money? Describe how you manage finances.
- » How are you affected by materialism?
- » Describe your active health and wellness practices.

STORM-SWEPT FAMILY

Storm-Swept Family
FIVE OF PENTACLES

Five of Pentacles

Beware of adopting a 'lack' mentality, as it will cause life's hardships to become the sole focus of your experience.

IN A READING

The *Five of Pentacles* signifies the destruction of redundant, old structures, bringing difficult lessons with it. These lessons relate to how we conduct our lives and rely on the material plane. In times of hardship, it's essential to remember that you're never truly alone. While loneliness can create a deep sense of isolation, engaging with a community—whether large or small—offers the support and connection you need. Reach out to those who care about you and allow yourself to lean into their support. Vulnerability is not a weakness but a pathway to strength and connection. While it's natural to feel overwhelmed by financial struggles or feelings of lack, focus on feeling grateful for what you have. Take small steps to regain stability, whether creating a budget, seeking assistance, or exploring new opportunities. Trust in your resilience and resourcefulness. You've overcome challenges before and have the inner strength to do so again. Stay open to unexpected blessings and opportunities that may arise amidst adversity. Above all, be gentle with yourself during this time. Practise self-care and compassion as you navigate through difficulties. This period is temporary, and with patience, perseverance, and a willingness to seek help when needed, you will emerge stronger and more resilient than ever before.

Reversed

You are beginning to move beyond financial burdens or material hardship. Where once there may have been insecurity or fear of lack, the *Five of Pentacles* reversed signals that the tide is starting to turn. You've found the strength to ask for help, or circumstances are finally shifting in your favour. As you release old patterns of scarcity and pride, there's room for renewal, both materially and emotionally.

While your struggles may have worn on your spirit, healing is within reach. The worst is behind you, and now is the time to embrace new opportunities for growth and stability. Take a moment to reflect on what you've learned from this period of difficulty, and use those insights to rebuild a stronger foundation moving forward. Practices like mindfulness and gratitude can help align your focus, giving you greater clarity and peace. As you step out of the cold and into the warmth of support—whether from loved ones, community, or even your own inner strength—trust that this is a time for restoration. Let go of past fears and move forward with hope and renewed energy.

Narrative

There comes a time when we must all weather the storms of life. Such a time came for this once-proud family. They had felt at home in a state of plenty, never having to worry about food, water, shelter, and the general—and sometimes lavish—comfort that such security brings. But all good things must end as the cycle of life moves in its unbiased rhythm. As wars over lands and gods raged, yesterday's resources became depleted. People across the land were forced from their homes to brave the dangerous roads in search of sanctuary. Many were pushed far from their homelands into places where the weather was freezing. The children and elderly struggled to navigate the foreboding landscapes. Eventually, this once-blessed family became detached from the migrating hoard and left to wander the cold woodland realm. At last, they found a nook in the forest, and the able-bodied of the bunch began work on a haphazard shelter strong enough to weather the storm. Little did they realise they had found their way into the Grove of Plenty. Once the storm had passed, along with the cold mist, they would find that the emergency shelter would set the foundation for their new home in a place that met all their needs.

Correspondences

- » **Astrology:** Mercury in Taurus
- » **Major Arcana:** *V The Hierophant, XV The Devil*

Journal Prompts

- » When have you triumphed over hardship?
- » How important is financial security to you?
- » What does being frugal mean to you?
- » Have you ever gone without? If so, what did that experience lead to?

FEED THE BIRDS

Six of Pentacles

By fostering a culture of giving and compassion, you create a ripple effect of positivity and abundance that uplifts yourself and those around you.

IN A READING

The *Six of Pentacles* represents a time of gift-giving. Gifts can appear as a helping hand that makes you feel supported, acknowledged, and encouraged. Perhaps as a wealthy benefactor bankrolling your dreams. Or, it could be a small donation perfectly timed to help you gain what you need. Cast aside any prideful reflexes and accept the support offered with gratitude and an open heart. You know what you want and need — look for the support needed, take the necessary steps, and direct yourself to the desired outcomes. This includes supporting others when you are in a state of abundance. Giving and receiving resources leads to a thriving community. Shopping locally, volunteering, and donating are all ways you can help support your community and environment. Find a state of balance where you are in harmony with the flow of resources entering and leaving your life, and you will notice that harmony spreads beyond you.

Reversed

This card in reverse signifies finding ways to support and encourage yourself, because you can't always rely on outside support to achieve your dreams. It heralds a time of self-sufficiency, of being your own benefactor, and of investing your time and resources to meet your desired state of being. Only pride stands in the way of growth. Ferociously coveting your resources while observing others in a state of need is far from kind and will have far-reaching consequences. Turn your focus towards your own achievements and the unique set of skills that you alone possess that made everything possible. Do not dilute the magnitude of your achievements through self-deprecating sarcasm or constant inner-criticism. Own your accomplishments and celebrate each one for the prize that they are.

Narrative

There comes a time when our pride must be put aside to accept the support being offered. Kindness is a sacred gift deserved by many. It costs nothing to be kind, to offer an ear, shoulder, or assistance to another. We throw our crumbs to birds and they adore it, yet we throw our crumbs to humans and they are offended by it. Where does the balance lie?

Correspondences

» **Astrology:** Moon in Taurus

» **Major Arcana:** *VI The Lovers, XVI The Tower*

Journal Prompts

» When was the last time you donated any of your resources?

» Can you identify the differences between your wants and needs? Create a list to see where they cross over.

» Do you practise gratitude in your life? Describe your favourite gratitude practice.

» How does dealing with ungrateful individuals make you feel?

OAKLEY

Seven of Pentacles

Now is the time to reap the rewards of your hard work. You are in a strong position to expand your views and efforts. Doing so will assure growth and expansion.

IN A READING

The *Seven of Pentacles* is a sign of the harvest to come. You've put significant energy into a project, and now it's time to see the rewards begin to blossom. The more effort you invest, the more you'll gain. While this isn't the moment for full harvest, it indicates that your hard work will prove worthwhile. Perseverance will bring a bountiful return. Re-examine your position, methods, and motivations and ensure you are aligned with the harvest. Not all the multiple projects on the go will prove to be successful. Continuing to invest time and energy into them all will reduce your chances of succeeding in just one, so develop one plan above all others. Pause and reassess your strategy. List the pros and cons, and ask yourself where your particular set of skills would be best served to ensure even greater success. Culling your projects to focus on just one is not limiting, especially if you document your ideas for other projects. While it may be difficult for you to achieve everything at once, approaching your projects one at a time will prove more successful in the long run.

Reversed

The *Seven of Pentacles* reversed suggests something is preventing you from moving forward. This can be from an underlying fear of failure, which manifests as self-sabotage. Despite your desire for success, there's a tendency to start projects with enthusiasm but struggle to see your projects through to completion. Or you could be tempted to pursue goals not aligned with your true self, which leads to poor choices with far-reaching consequences. Pause and reassess. Take a moment to clearly define your goals and break them into manageable, actionable steps to make the path to success more attainable. Redirect your focus towards nurturing your creative side, which you've likely neglected. Reconnecting with your inner spark can bring inspiration and motivation back into your life, reigniting the passion that fuels your journey. By embracing your creativity, align with your authentic self and set the stage for true, soul-nourishing success. Overcoming the paralysis of indecision, you can only take meaningful strides towards your aspirations.

Narrative

Oakley had always been a hard worker. Since a baby, Oakley had demonstrated a quiet tenacity in all endeavours. As a young adult, Oakley approached the pastime of mushroom harvesting with a bit more rigour. Little did Oakley know that the demand for mushrooms in nearby regions had increased dramatically. Soon, visitors came to his family's cottage with offers to buy mushrooms. When Oakley asked the first such visitor what type of mushroom he wanted to purchase, they became so excited that they bought some of each type and returned to his home with news of a well-stocked mushroom supplier. Good news travels fast, and soon Oakley's pockets were lined with silver and gold. Oakley's family was gifted with livestock in exchange for rarer mushrooms. Oakley's reputation for being honest, hardworking, and professional made certain that Oakley was always the most sought-after of the mushroom harvesters.

Correspondences

- » **Astrology:** Saturn in Taurus
- » **Major Arcana:** *VII The Chariot, XVII The Star*

Journal Prompts

- » What have you planted that is now ready for harvest?
- » What do the words 'harvest' and 'reap' suggest?
- » Describe how you approach the completion of your tasks.
- » Would you say you are hard-working? Describe your work ethic.

The Sacred Smith
EIGHT OF PENTACLES

THE SACRED SMITH

Eight of Pentacles

Embrace discipline and focus to refine your skills. Repetition breeds mastery.

In a Reading

The *Eight of Pentacles* signifies a skilled craftsperson possessing a healthy dose of perfectionism. Focus on the matter at hand and seek methods to refine your approach to your work. Perhaps a much more detail-oriented approach is necessary, so developing a more intelligent work structure will help you achieve your goals in a timely fashion. Don't be surprised if this leads to a profound recognition of your life's path. For this reason, listen to your inner voice, but do not allow yourself to be ruled by it — prudence is the ideal approach. Surrender to the call of your vocation. This is particularly true for those who have knowingly or unknowingly resisted it. Your talents are unique and worth nurturing, and through these, you become the master of your destiny.

Reversed

When the *Eight of Pentacles* is reversed, it suggests your hands have been idle for too long, perhaps due to fatigue after over-exerting yourself. Sustaining high levels of work and commitment isn't possible, and pushing beyond your limits may leave you feeling unmotivated and stuck. Having become overly self-absorbed in your situation, now is the ideal time to step back and regain perspective. Prevent burnout by nurturing your body, mind, and spirit — this is essential to your wellbeing. Prioritise rest, explore activities that bring joy, and reconnect with supportive people or practices. Doing so will reawaken your energy and motivation, helping you find clarity and purpose again. By taking time to care for yourself, you'll restore balance and build resilience. Trust that you have the strength to reawaken your lifeforce and, with it, your motivation.

Narrative

Since she was a babe, Sable sat in awe of her father's skill. Her father was a well-known smith who was thought to be able to bend the will of iron. His customers came from all parts of the world. However, he was a selective man. He was often heard asking rather odd questions, questions that were designed to assess their honour. If satisfied, he would offer his services. If unsatisfied, he would send them packing. All the while, Sable watched on in awe and respect for her noble father. As she grew, her desire became clear. Much to her mother's dismay, she showed little interest in what were then considered feminine pursuits. No, Sable wanted to follow in her dad's footsteps and become a smith. But, to succeed in her ambition, she would have to show more promise than any other. And so began her journey towards mastery, a journey that would take years. She would walk the road of magic and mysticism to become the greatest Sacred Smith known to the lands.

Correspondences

- **Astrology:** Sun in Virgo
- **Major Arcana:** *VIII Strength, XVIII The Moon*

Journal Prompts

- Do you know the feeling of being utterly obsessed with a project? Describe the project.
- Describe your greatest talent.
- What does being detail-oriented mean to you?
- Do you believe that hard work pays off? What is one of your favourite work mottos?

THE LADY OF FLOWERS

Nine of Pentacles

The Lady of Flowers
NINE OF PENTACLES

It is time for you to bloom and experience growth, creativity, and satisfaction. Embrace joy and, with it, a welcome sense of security and confidence.

IN A READING

The *Nine of Pentacles* signifies a time of brilliant abundance. The resources you have worked hard to secure are now available, and a time of harmony and joy is upon you. This card speaks to all types of material gain, so of course, you will feel plentiful and be blessed with the freedom to enjoy the rewards of your efforts. It also highlights the importance of the real jewels in your life — all that is more important and usually immaterial, like family, friends, and good health.

Harness this energy to enhance your creativity and embrace a strong urge to share your newfound visionary expressions with the world. Explore your imaginative potential, engage in artistic endeavours, and let your innovative ideas flow freely. By doing so, you connect with others in meaningful ways and make a significant impact with your creative contributions. Embrace happiness in your life, choose what is right for you in each moment, and be satisfied with that decision. Prioritising your needs and happiness is an act of self-love and kindness that helps to be nurtured every so often. This prevents feeling depleted and burnt out and ensures continued sustained energy to create, create, create.

Reversed

The reversed version of this card symbolises a scarcity of resources and the worries and stress associated with that. It signifies a time when talent and creativity are stifled. There may be an abundance of potential, but you are unable to express the effects because of the stagnation, which leads to feeling resentful and restricted. You need the sharp relief of balance. Moderate your expenditure now to ensure you are not giving out more than you are taking in. Make your resources work for you at this time. Budgeting and planning are great allies. These interventions will be of tremendous benefit to you because you can plan ahead at a glance and not be left short-changed.

Narrative

The Lady of Flowers blossoms and dances in an ecstatic existence. Power is her beauty, and she radiates resplendently. She is encumbered by nothing, free to express herself through dance, and her dances are exquisite, unbridled, and ecstatic. Her dances are a real, honest celebration of the sovereign self. No one can look away from nature's dancer. She is a gift to be seen, and witnessing her is perhaps one of the most incredible omens. She is a pure expression of life, sacred in all ways.

Correspondences

- **Astrology:** Venus in Virgo
- **Major Arcana:** *IX The Hermit, XIX The Sun*

Journal Prompts

- What does the term 'blossoming' mean to you?
- Describe a time in your life when you found yourself in a true abundance.
- Describe how you react in the face of restrictions.
- How do you believe that fortune favours the bold?

COMMUNITY

Ten of Pentacles

Your past efforts have culminated in a season of fruitful abundance. Embrace a sense of gratitude for all that you have achieved.

IN A READING

The *Ten of Pentacles* represents a time of prolonged and lasting happiness — an era of security, both in your resources and familial attachments. Your home's order and structure bring a sense of peace and grounded harmony. Your attention shifts from wealth and material possessions to personal interconnectedness and the nurturing of meaningful relationships.

This is a card of completion, of goals achieved, and of projects running their fruitful course. A great deal of work and commitment has been invested. Now is the time to enjoy the spoils and celebrate this with your loved ones. The solid grounding sustains you for the next chapter of your life. Take this opportunity to breathe deeply and express gratitude for your achievements. Invest a little time and energy in nurturing your physical body through conscious nutrition and healthy movement. Honour your physical vessel so that it may support you fully in all aspects of life. Caring for your body ensures it can sustain your energy, creativity, and wellbeing.

Reversed

Your house is out of order, and the *Ten of Pentacles* reversed suggests it may be due to your idle efforts. Maybe you desired a particular stature but lost focus and drive in your efforts to achieve it. Or perhaps you've been driven by greed all this time. Whatever it is, harmony is lacking in areas, and as such, things are out of balance. Find the root cause that initially propelled you on your path and reconnect with the purity of it. Stop letting yourself be ruled by a lack of resources, as this limits your imagination and blinds you to any creative solutions. Look for alternative perspectives. You have more at your disposal than you realise. Take a step back and allow yourself to see the bigger picture. Remember, there are always more ways than one to approach a situation and ensure its success. Innovation is seldom the most direct route. It may be time to step outside the box and follow your gut instincts. Take a moment to pause and reflect to remember who you are and what you are truly working towards. Lean into the love and support of your family and friends. Those who know you well are invaluable in helping you reignite the original spark that motivated you to get to work.

Narrative

This family nurtures one another. They offer the support necessary for success to prevail. The work of one is the work of all, and no hand lies idle in the face of a project. This family is capable, proud, nurturing, and loving. Under such a support system, all thrive. They are as conventional as they are unconventional. Their uniqueness is part of their abundant skill set. In this family, a pig is a kindred member of the household. So, too, is the duck. For them, life in all its forms matters. They understand that the rich resources they have secured are not some trifling thing. They understand it's a by-product of striving to live a complete life, emphasising honouring the flow of nature and living in harmony with it.

Correspondences

» **Astrology:** Mercury in Virgo
» **Major Arcana:** *X The Wheel of Fortune, XX Judgement*

Journal Prompts

» What does the word 'dynasty' bring to mind?
» Describe your family unit.
» How would you say your family is conventional or unconventional?
» Describe your favourite family gathering.

DIONYSUS
Page of Pentacles

Guided by spirited diligence, the wise balance labour with leisure, threading a path through life that is both pragmatic and indulgent, respectful yet free-spirited.

IN A READING

The *Page of Pentacles* embodies an unusual level of practicality. It's time to embark on a course of study to assist you in increasing a skill relevant to your vocation. Your next steps should be practical and methodical. Patience is required for this next stage. Grounding and centring yourself before decision-making is beneficial, allowing you to call back your energy and operate from a position of wholeness. Kick off your shoes and feel the solidity of the earth beneath the soft pads of your feet. With each deep breath you take, draw the raw and nurturing energy of the earth into yourself, feeling the energy of life coursing through your subtle body. Placing one hand on your heart and the other on your abdomen, visualise your scattered energy gathering and concentrating at the solar plexus. Imagine this bright, warm energy growing brighter and warmer with each breath. Now, it is time to reclaim your energy. Visualise the energy you've left with other people or places returning to you, merging with the light at your core. Each time you inhale, this light becomes brighter and more vibrant, filling you with a sense of completeness and tranquillity.

As a Person

The grounded Page represents a pragmatic individual. A steady and helpful hand, he never shies away from hard work and is often the first person called on to help start a project. His deliberate nature and practical approach in all situations breeds an air of quiet confidence. With a healthy love of knowledge, he constantly gains insights from life and never sees himself as an expert. This keeps him grounded and humble. People who embody this archetype tend to be attractive and have warm and nurturing personalities. They genuinely listen when others speak, focusing their full attention on the conversation at hand. Making others feel genuinely heard is a natural part of their energy, so they often make excellent friends and confidants.

However, a downside to this personality can be a judgemental undertone. If they disagree with someone's actions, they won't hesitate to express their opinion, often quite bluntly. Though this directness might come across as harsh, they firmly believe that honesty is the best policy and will encourage others to practise the same level of transparency, even if it leads to disagreements.

Reversed

The *Page of Pentacles* reversed suggests difficulty in learning, such as experiencing a scattered mind and struggle to maintain focus. This creates insecurity and embarrassment, often masked by distracting or harmful behaviours like hedonism and excess. These tendencies are usually distracting from the problem at hand. You may also find yourself judgemental and overly focused on others' faults instead of your own. Honest self-reflection is essential. Take a step back and slow down. Rather than indulging in distractions, focus on grounding yourself and addressing the root cause of your scattered energy. A structured approach will help you set small, manageable goals and tackle them individually. This will rebuild your confidence and sense of control. It's also essential to be kind to yourself — everyone has moments of difficulty, and no one is immune to struggle.

So take a moment to reconnect with your purpose and allow yourself the necessary time to regroup and refocus. During this time of inward focus, avoid comparing your own unique journey to the journey of others. Instead, embrace the lessons found in your own path and honour these lessons to the best of your ability. With patience and persistence, you can regain your footing.

This reversed card can also indicate individuals who show little to no respect for the planet, engaging in wasteful consumption and unsustainable habits. Become mindful of how your actions impact the environment. Consider small but meaningful steps to reduce waste and be more conscious of your consumption. Simple changes, like recycling, cutting down on single-use plastics, or supporting sustainable practices, can help you realign with a more balanced, responsible way of living. Respecting the natural environment benefits the planet and creates a deeper connection to nature, and fosters a sense of personal responsibility.

Narrative

Dionysus is a man of the earth, at peace in the green landscapes. From there, he draws a tremendous amount of power, both sensual and seductive in nature. But make no mistake — while he may be incredibly alluring, he is also of nature, grounded, and centred. He is in possession of a patient knowing. He has spent many a day leaning against the knowledgeable trunks of trees, with his fingers deep in the earth, trying to understand better what it means to be fertile. His greatest mentor is the planet itself. He gains pleasure from observing the changes in cycles and seeks to harmonise with the sequences to better understand his own nature. He's a perpetual student. He studies efficiently, examines, cooperates with, and facilitates the green world in any way he can. He is a faithful steward of the natural environment.

Correspondences

» **Astrology:** Virgo

» **Elemental Combinations:** Earth of Earth

Journal Prompts

» If you could partake in a course of study, what would it be?

» How practical do you think you are?

» In what ways do you demonstrate eco-conscious behaviours and strategies?

» What steps could you take to become more eco-friendly in your day-to-day life?

Lilith
KNIGHT OF PENTACLES

LILITH

Knight of Pentacles

Embrace the strength of simplicity and let loyalty guide you, for true prosperity is achieved through steadfastness and patience.

IN A READING

The *Knight of Pentacles* heralds a time of increased responsibility and a phase of slow-unfurling momentum. Welcome this as part of your evolution, and feel free to be ambitious and face your challenges head-on. When seeking to achieve your goals, act purposefully and be patient — steady progress will propel you forward. For this reason, it is important to care for your body. Include more movement into your practical daily routine. For example, you could take the stairs instead of the elevator, use a bike instead of a car, walk as often as possible, and breathe in the fresh air around you. Caring for your physical body is a sacred act of love and kindness for yourself. Take a moment to ground yourself and lay the foundations for your intentions. Once you feel sure and steady, take the appropriate actions to achieve your goal. Adopting healthier habits and moving forward through grounded and inspired actions daily invites beautiful changes in your life that help you pave your way to a happier and healthier version of yourself.

As a Person

This seductive Knight represents an incredibly attractive and charismatic character. She possesses a healthy vanity, dressing well, smelling good, and caring for her physical body. She is a creature of habit and an animal and nature lover at heart, enjoying the great outdoors and preferring time in nature to time in shopping centres, clubs, or bars.

She despises cages. Her best work is when she feels free — mostly outside. For this reason, she is eco-friendly and prefers natural minimalism. Her possessions pale compared to others, but she has the best of everything she truly needs. She does not believe in excess, nor does she desire anything more than is actually required.

Reversed

The reversed version of this card generally signifies a period of stagnation, triggering an unimaginative streak or lack of movement in your life. Where there was once a great deal of inspiration and motivation, there is now a sense of apathy, restlessness, and indolence. Brush off the dust and embrace a new, more dynamic approach. Get out of your own head. Go outside, go for a walk, and engage in conversation with strangers where safe and possible. Let go of stubbornness and worry from your mind by inviting in new experiences that you find activating and inspiring. Engaging in new activities helps you activate a growth mindset, which enables you to awaken your creativity. By keeping your life dynamic and engaging, you create room for happiness and satisfaction to enter your life.

Narrative

Lilith speaks the primal language of the serpentine force, a gift bestowed upon her since her youth. Enchanted by the reptilian world, she understands their every hiss and whisper, a bond that defies the laws of nature. Many have cast their gaze upon her, believing her to be under the dominion of the serpentine power. Yet, they knew not the truth — Lilith does not submit to the serpents; she commands them. They coil at her feet, awaiting her call, responding to her every emotion.

When sadness enveloped her, they came. When rage consumed her, they rose in fury. When the world misunderstood her, the serpents struck at her adversaries without hesitation. The world soon learned that Lilith is no mere mortal force. She is the embodiment of the primal, a being whose wrath should not be tested. Neither man nor woman dares cross one who wields the serpents' will, for Lilith is an elemental power unlike any other.

Correspondences

- » **Astrology:** Virgo
- » **Elemental Combinations:** Air of Earth

Journal Prompts

- » Where do you go when you want to feel grounded?
- » Where do you most feel at home?
- » Describe your stubborn streak.
- » What is your cure for the times when you feel unimaginative?

Baba Yaga
QUEEN OF PENTACLES

BABA YAGA

Queen of Pentacles

Indulge your senses and luxuriate in the beauty of the natural world. Step into the archetype of the Divine Feminine and honour the sensuality of your physical body.

IN A READING

The *Queen of Pentacles* symbolises a period of grounded creation and practical empowerment. She invites you to embrace your sovereignty while staying deeply connected to the material world. In this sense, generosity is another key theme. This card appears when you feel you need to nurture yourself, improve your physical wellbeing, or create greater comfort in your life.

To achieve balance, prioritise self-care through nourishing food, proper rest, and a regular exercise routine. Simple rituals like mindful relaxation or enjoying small luxuries can make you feel valued and centred. Balance giving and receiving by sharing your time, resources, or support with others. This cycle of abundance strengthens connections and brings deeper fulfilment into your life. In financial matters, focus on planning and consistent action — whether you're reaping the rewards of hard work or planting seeds for future success. By cultivating excellence and attention to detail in everything you do, you ensure meaningful growth and lasting security. Trust in your ability to create a life of balance and abundance.

As a Person

This archetype is practical in her approach to her appearance. She prefers to clock her attributes and does not wish to be judged by her appearance alone. She is authentic and natural and prefers to carry a curio or two with her wherever she goes. She places greater importance on her physical health than engaging in vain practices or attaining an impossible beauty standard. Instead, she is solid and grounded in her presence, and these qualities command respect. This Queen is a generous soul with a giving nature. While she does not suffer a fool, she has an uncanny knack for seeing through illusions and, with it, the lies of others. She feels the truth and can sniff out ulterior motives.

The Queen of the earth element is the type of individual who possesses the mythical 'Midas touch'. She has a natural affinity for good business and does not hesitate when she sees an opportunity for future growth. Her approach is all about the end game, and she spends no time attempting to secure the quick buck. She is naturally resourceful, and it is for this reason that she is worth her weight in gold. She is genuinely feminine and incredibly warm and loving. When she loves you, she will love you forever. Cross her, however, and hell hath no fury.

Reversed

The reversed *Queen of Pentacles* suggests an imbalance rooted in materialism, vanity, and rigid thinking that can lead to inflexibility and selfishness. It manifests as feeling overwhelmed by the pressure to acquire more, believing happiness lies in possessions. It causes you to be too rigid in your thinking, and acting out of fear of change can block personal growth. It's time to reassess your priorities and differentiate between wants and needs. Cultivate a mindset of curiosity and openness — learn from others, ask questions, and embrace new perspectives. Take control of your financial situation. Acts of self-love, including nurturing your emotional and feminine qualities, can also help restore balance Because this reversed card highlights the impact of unhealthy vanity, it is a reminder that beauty and worth come from within. Relationships thrive when nurtured with care and genuine attention. By realigning your values and reconnecting with what truly matters, you can find fulfilment that extends beyond the material world.

Narrative

She is as ancient as time itself — patient, knowing, wise, and perpetually misunderstood. For this reason, she was driven away from her people to live in peace at the edge of an ancient forest. Truth be told, she expected such treatment. She understood that what humanity does not understand, it fears. She had no desire to live amongst a community that simply did not understand, nor did they show signs of wanting to learn.

She agreed to move out into the ancient forest and live her own way. She rather preferred that option, frankly. She understood that by choosing such a life, people would talk. They would speak of her strangeness and her appearance, but more than that, they would talk of her magic. She also knew that she would be sought out for her skills — the very skills that saw her removed from society. She could see it, clear as day. They would walk the wooded path under cover of night, with desperation in their pounding hearts. They would come with pockets full of silver, and fear coursing through their veins. And there, in her rickety cottage, they would meet her. There, they would meet the Baba Yaga.

Correspondences

- » **Astrology:** Taurus
- » **Elemental Combinations:** Water of Earth

Journal Prompts

- » What does 'healthy vanity' mean to you?
- » Describe a moment in your life where you felt the most sensual.
- » What does 'fertility' mean to you?
- » Looking through the eyes of a child, describe your temperament.

The Green Man
KING OF PENTACLES

THE GREEN MAN

King of Pentacles

Take up the mantle of power and manage your resources as though you were a monarch.

IN A READING

The *King of Pentacles* represents a mastery over resources, urging you to take full advantage of what you have to foster growth, prosperity, and stability. It emphasises the importance of tending to your 'kingdom'—finances, career, or personal life—through consistent care and thoughtful actions. Hard work, reliability, and self-respect are the cornerstones of enduring success. By respecting yourself, you naturally extend that respect towards others.

Thus, share your abundance by supporting loved ones, offering guidance, or building a sense of community. True mastery lies not just in self-sufficiency but in creating an environment where others thrive alongside you. By focusing on wise, sustainable choices—whether financial independence or eco-conscious living—you create a life of lasting comfort and security. When you embrace both stewardship and generosity, you establish a legacy of abundance and fulfilment for yourself and those around you.

As a Person

This grounded, earthy King represents a loyal, pragmatic, and influential individual who prioritises his friends and family. Hands-on and willing to put in hours of physical labour, he ensures the harmony of his home by building and creating with his bare hands. He encourages others to contribute their fair share to the success of any project. As an efficient worker, he manages resources well and is generous, never shying away from an investment—even risky ones—after thorough research. As an excellent provider and loving partner, he combines natural charm with good conversational skills, though he prefers meaningful discussions over idle chitchat. Honest and good-natured, with a beautiful sense of humour, he can sometimes be the life of the party, attracting the spotlight due to his natural demeanour and pleasing appearance.

Reversed

The reversed *King of Pentacles* suggests a lack of direction and stubbornness in addressing your challenges, leading to frustration and internal lethargy. If you feel overwhelmed or stuck, now is the time to reassess your approach. Start by identifying where you've become rigid in your thinking or unwilling to adapt. Are you holding on to old habits or unrealistic expectations? A good way to start is by journalling or seeking input from someone you trust to help break through your mental block.

The underlying anger or frustration you feel may stem from this stagnation. To deal with these emotions, practise mindfulness to observe and acknowledge your feelings without judgement. Consider physical activities like exercise or yoga to release built-up tension. If you feel disconnected from what matters, create a simple action plan to realign your priorities. Write down what's truly important to you right now and break down steps to reconnect with those goals. Shifting your mindset and refocusing your energy will restore balance and gain a clearer path forward. Embrace flexibility and adaptability, knowing this approach will lead you towards personal growth and a more grounded sense of direction.

Narrative

The Green Man is a primal force to be reckoned with. His magic and majesty are the wild heart that beats through every sentient creature. Holding sway over the primal force surging through all creation, he is the roar, the tooth, the blood, and the venom.

No one knows how this ancient being came to be. Some say he is a shadow cast by trees. Others that he is the cave dweller who lives in the centre of the earth, forever caressing his other half, the Great Mother.

Humans will pray to him; they will pray to be reminded of the majesty and sovereignty inside them. His wild nature embodies life, reminding everyone of their beating hearts and urging them to run wild and free.

Correspondences

- » **Astrology:** Capricorn
- » **Elemental Combinations:** Fire of Earth

Journal Prompts

- » Describe your kingdom.

- » Describe a time in your life when you were a provider.
- » Describe a time in your life when you were unnecessarily insensitive.
- » How do you relate to the *King of Pentacles*?

About the Author

Avalon Cameron is a hereditary Brazilian Witch, now residing off-grid in the serene wilderness of Southern Tasmania, Australia, with her beautiful family. Deeply rooted in her Brazilian ancestry, Avalon practises a sacred and ancestral form of magic, specialising in folk magic, spirit work, and tarot. As a professional tarot reader, she boasts an impressive collection of tarot and oracle decks, with a preference for the Smith–Waite system.

With decades of experience, Avalon reads the cards with ritualistic precision, offering grounded and inspiring insights. A trailblazer in the tarot community, she created the unique first edition of the *Bonestone & Earthflesh Tarot* deck live on YouTube, a first of its kind.

Avalon is not just a tarot expert; she imparts wisdom to those seeking a magically infused, soul-filled life.

Connect with Avalon at: ***avaloncameron.com***

About the Artist

Ana Tourian is an internationally known tarot artist and creator whose works include *Hidden Waters Tarot*, *Oracle of Echoes*, *Clair de Lune Lenormand*, and *The Abyss Tarot*, to name but a few.

She is an avid tarot lover and has been reading tarot for over twenty years with grace, respect, and proficiency.

Ana holds a BFA in Painting and Drawing and an MFA in Communication Packaging Design from Pratt Institute, NY. When she's not creating a new divination deck, Ana can be found sculpting or hiking.

She lives with her two children, her husband, and her dog, Charley, in New Jersey.

You can reach Ana at: ***anatourianart.com***

Also available from *Blue Angel Publishing*

THE BADDELEY TAROT

JAKE BADDELEY

A Journey of Wisdom, Myth and Transformation

The Baddeley Tarot invites you to explore an ancient system that has guided seekers for centuries, drawing upon the forbidden esoteric wisdom of the past. Deeply researched and richly layered, this deck connects the symbolism of early tarots with the philosophies and spirit of the Renaissance era. The illustrations by Jake Baddeley, inspired by the techniques of Renaissance masters, weave multiple layers of meaning, creating a tarot deck that speaks to both the intellect and the spirit.

78 cards + 368-page colour guidebook. ISBN: 978-1-922574-34-3

Also available from *Blue Angel Publishing*

THE WILD WITCH ORACLE

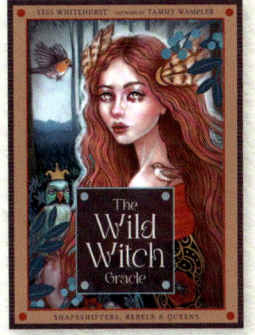

TESS WHITEHURST
ARTWORK BY TAMMY WAMPLER

Shapeshifters, Rebels & Queens

The brave spirits of this deck are here to call you back to your native wildness: to remind you that you are wise, independent, empowered, and free.

Featuring 44 bold heroines voiced by author Tess Whitehurst and beautifully illustrated by artist Tammy Wampler, *The Wild Witch Oracle* delivers messages that enliven your courage to create a life that's truly authentic. From astrological goddesses to nature sprites, faerie queens to historical monarchs, the supernatural and the human collide, awakening your innate divine powers.

44 cards + 160-page colour guidebook. ISBN: 978-1-922574-39-8

Also available from *Blue Angel Publishing*

SOUL REFLECTIONS TAROT

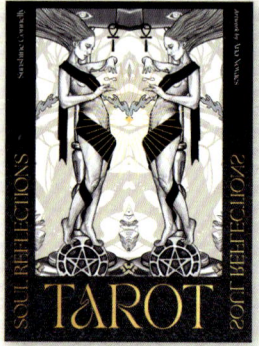

SUNSHINE CONNELLY
ARTWORK BY ANA NOVAES

Soul Reflections Tarot is your invitation to a journey of personal transformation grounded in the practice of Soul Mirroring. Created by Sunshine Connelly and illustrated by Ana Novaes, this deck is a companion to their best-selling *Soul Mirror Oracle*. Using the framework of Tarot, it combines intuitive wisdom and stunning artwork to help you reflect, heal, and grow. This deck encourages you to observe emotions, experiences, and patterns as opportunities for growth.

Discover your potential to heal and evolve, one card at a time.

78 cards + 288-page colour guidebook. ISBN: 978-1-922574-40-4

Also available from *Blue Angel Publishing*

LIGHT IN THE DARKNESS ORACLE

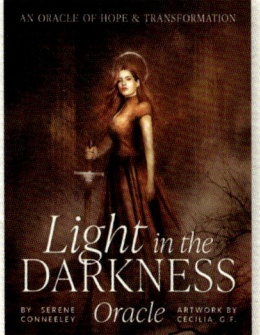

SERENE CONNEELEY
ARTWORK BY CECILIA G.F.

An Oracle of Hope and Transformation

Welcome to a place of warmth and wonder. This 44-card oracle deck invites you to embrace the balance of light and shadow within yourself, discovering the strength, wisdom and magic that reside in your heart. Written by Serene Conneeley *(Practical Magic)* and featuring luminous artwork by Cecilia G.F., *Light in the Darkness* is your companion and confidante through life's twists and shades — helping you release burdens, navigate challenges and uncover the boundless hidden truths you already hold.

3. The Gift of Yes   7. Stop the Spiral   15. Let Down Your Guard

44 cards + 192-page colour guidebook. ISBN: 978-1-922574-51-0

BLUE ANGEL®
PUBLISHING

For more information on this or any other Blue Angel Publishing release, please visit our website at:

www.blueangelonline.com